WHAT
WHEN SOM

About the author

Paul Harris is the business manager of a firm of funeral directors in Salisbury. He has been conducting funerals for over 30 years, has organised seminars on various subjects, including bereavement care, and writes regularly for *Funerals* magazine and other local and national periodicals.

WHAT TO DO
WHEN SOMEONE DIES

PAUL HARRIS

CONSUMERS' ASSOCIATION

Which? Books are commissioned and researched by
The Association for Consumer Research and published by
Consumers' Association, 2 Marylebone Road, NW1 4DF
Distributed by the Penguin Group
Penguin Books Ltd, 27 Wrights Lane, London W8 5TZ

First edition April 1967
Amended reprint October 1989
Revised edition October 1991
Amended reprint September 1992
New edition April 1994

Based on *What to Do When Someone Dies* (Consumers' Association);
text revised and new material written by Paul Harris; Scottish sections
revised by David Nichols

British Library Cataloguing in Publication Data

Rev. ed.–('Which?' Consumer Guides)
I. Harris, Paul II. Nichols, David
III. Series
363.750941
ISBN 0 85202 515 7

Cover photographs by courtesy of Sally and Richard Greenhill and
The Geoffrey Goode Picture Collection

Photoset by Paston Press Ltd, Loddon, Norfolk
Printed and bound in Great Britain by Clays Ltd, St Ives plc

CONTENTS

FOREWORD

SINCE 1967, this book has helped countless thousands of readers to make the necessary arrangements at what, for most of them, will have been a very difficult time. For those who have never before had to deal with the practical arrangements that must be made after a death we explain how to go about getting a doctor's certificate, registering the death, deciding whether to bury or cremate, choosing a funeral director and coffin, putting notices in the papers, selecting the form of service and claiming any state benefits due. We explain the function of people with whom they will come in contact, often for the first time – the doctor, registrar, funeral director, clergyman, cemetery or crematorium officials, Department of Social Security officials and, in some cases, the police and the coroner. However, it is the executor or nearest relative who has to make the decisions; *What to Do When Someone Dies* describes what needs to be done, when, and how to set about it.

In this edition, for the first time, we explain the practicalities of burials arranged without the services of a funeral director and we also look at humanist and other non-Christian funerals. We examine briefly the personal aspects of death and bereavement; some understanding of the normal grief processes helps us to gauge and perhaps make allowances for the feeling of others and aids us in making rational decisions.

To give you an idea of how much you should expect to pay for a burial or cremation we quote prices (dated where possible).

However, prices vary considerably and should be checked carefully in the local area.

Note Addresses and telephone numbers for those organisations marked with an asterisk (★) can be found in the address section at the back of the book.

CHAPTER 1

DEATH

YOU MAY discover someone apparently dead, and it can be difficult to tell whether he or she really is dead or not. For instance, someone rescued from water may appear not to breathe, yet might be revived by artificial respiration or the 'kiss of life'.

The body temperature drops at the rate of one or two degrees centigrade an hour for the first few hours after death, so someone who has been dead for an hour or so is appreciably colder than normal. The extremities – feet and hands – get cold first. But very low body temperature alone is not a sure sign of death because comatose or unconscious people can also seem abnormally cold.

If there is any doubt whether someone is dead, treat him or her as being still alive.

Telling the doctor

The first thing to do is to call the doctor. If you do not know how or where to get hold of a doctor, dial 999 for the emergency ambulance service. If there is any doubt at all as to whether the person has actually died, call the doctor immediately. However, if the doctor has been in regular attendance and the person concerned has been expected to die, there is no need to disturb the doctor in the middle of the night: early the next morning will be sufficient.

Ask whether the doctor is going to come. If the death has been peaceful and expected, the doctor may not feel it necessary to come, or at least not straight away. If the doctor does not intend coming, ask his or her permission for a funeral director to remove the body, which cannot be done otherwise. If a decision has already been made that the funeral will involve cremation, you should tell the doctor at this point as papers will need to be prepared which will involve the doctor in examining the body and arranging for another doctor to perform a similar examination. Some doctors make a point of seeing the body of every patient who has died as soon as is convenient. However, the doctor may prefer to examine the deceased at the funeral director's mortuary, in which case (with the doctor's permission) the body may be removed by the appropriate funeral director.

Laying out the body

The initial preparation of the body for burial or cremation is called **laying out**; if this is done by a nurse or in hospital it will be referred to as 'last offices', while a funeral director will refer to it as 'first offices' (because it is the last service performed for the deceased by the medical profession and the first by the funeral director). This involves washing and tidying the body, closing the eyelids and ensuring that the jaw remains closed. The hair is tidied and sometimes washed, the arms and legs are straightened and, if necessary, the body's orifices are stopped with cotton wool. A man may need to be shaved as the hair continues to grow for some time after death. If laying out is done by a funeral director, the body will be dressed ready for the funeral, either in a funeral gown or, if preferred by the relatives, in everyday clothes.

There is a small but growing tendency for the family to arrange and conduct funerals for deceased relatives – see 'Arranging a funeral without a funeral director', **Chapter 14**. In this case, you can do the laying out yourself at home. Most people still prefer to hand over funeral arrangements to a funeral director, who will then attend to the laying out. This may be done at home, if preferred; a funeral director will not normally charge extra for this service within working hours, but will usually prefer to attend to the deceased at his or her mortuary. Many hospitals now provide only a basic laying out service, leaving the majority to be done by the funeral director.

Rigor mortis is a stiffening of the muscles, which usually begins within about six hours after death and gradually extends over the whole body in about 24 hours; after this it usually begins to wear off. Rigor mortis is less pronounced in the body of an elderly person.

When someone has been dead for half an hour or more, parts of the skin often begin to discolour with purple/black patches. This is called **hypostasis**, or post mortem staining, and is due to blood settling in the body due to the action of gravity.

If someone has died at home in bed, quietly and expectedly, it is perfectly in order to rearrange the body and tidy the room. If, however, someone collapses and dies unexpectedly, or a dead body is discovered in unusual circumstances, you must summon the doctor immediately and do as little as possible until he or she comes. Do not move the body unless there are exceptional circumstances, for example, if someone collapses and dies while crossing a road or at the top of a flight of stairs.

Calling the police

If you think that death appears to have been caused by an accident or violence, or to have occurred in other non-natural or suspicious circumstances, you should inform the police at once.

Do not touch or move anything in the room, nor allow anyone else to do so, until the police say that you may. The police will almost certainly want to take statements from anyone who was with the deceased when he or she died, or who discovered the body, but no one is obliged to give a statement to the police. If there is an inquest later, anyone who has made a statement may be called as a witness, as may any person whom the coroner believes may be able to give information about the death.

If a body cannot be identified immediately, the police circulate a description in police journals, and occasionally to the general press, too. Anyone who might be able to identify the body usually has to go to the mortuary with the police.

If the police are called and no relative or other person responsible is immediately available, the police take possession of any cash or valuables. As a general rule, this property is given up to whoever can later prove the right to it. The police also take away any article which may have a bearing on the cause of death – a letter or bottle of pills, for example – in case this is needed by the coroner.

Medical certificate of the cause of death

Every death that occurs in the UK must be registered at the local registrar's office within five days (see **Chapter 2**) and the registrar will require a certificate providing medical evidence of the cause of death. Normally, the doctor who has been attending the deceased will sign the certificate, but he or she cannot do so if there is any doubt whatsoever about the actual cause of death.

If the doctor knows the cause of death, he or she will provide the relatives with a certificate which states (to the best of the doctor's knowledge) the cause or causes of death, the last date on which he or she saw the patient alive and whether or not a doctor has seen the body since death occurred. This will usually be given to the family in a sealed envelope, together with a small form which gives basic details about registering the death. No charge is made for this certificate.

If the doctor is uncertain for any reason about the actual cause of death or has not seen the patient within a period of 14 days before death occurred, he or she cannot sign the death certificate. In such cases the coroner must be informed (see **Chapter 6**) – the coroner's officer will normally contact the family and explain procedures. The body will then be taken to the coroner's mortuary (usually at a local hospital) where the cause of death will be investigated, which may or may not involve a post mortem examination.

In normal cases where the doctor signs the medical certificate of the cause of death, this must be taken to the registrar's office in the district or sub-district in which the death occurred. In some circumstances, the doctor may send the certificate on to the registrar.

CHAPTER 2

REGISTERING THE DEATH

In this country, a death should be registered within five days of it happening. Registration can be delayed for a further nine days provided the registrar receives, in writing, confirmation that a medical certificate of the cause of death has been signed by the doctor.

Under English law, all deaths must be registered in the registration sub-district in which they took place or in which the body was found. A list of names, addresses and telephone numbers of local registrars of births and deaths is usually displayed in doctors' surgeries and in public libraries and other public buildings, together with their office hours and a description of the sub-district they cover.

Usually, whoever is giving the information goes in person to the registrar's office. Very few registration districts have an appointment system; normally you just go along during the registrar's office hours and wait until he or she is free to see you.

The informant

When a medical certificate of the cause of death is completed by a doctor, he or she must also complete that part of it which provides information for the informant or person informing the registrar of the details of the death which has occurred.

One side of the form is entitled 'notice to informant' and provides details of the information which the registrar will require:

- the date and place of death
- the full name and surname of the deceased (and the maiden name if the deceased was a married woman)
- the date and place of birth of the deceased
- the occupation of the deceased (and husband's name and occupation if the deceased was a married woman or widow)
- the usual address of the deceased
- whether the deceased was in receipt of a pension or allowance from public funds
- if the deceased was married, the date of birth of the surviving partner.

The form also states that the deceased's medical card should be taken and given to the registrar.

The other side of the form provides details of those who are qualified to act as informants. If the death has occurred inside a house or public building, any of the following may register the death:

- a relative of the deceased who was present at the death
- a relative of the deceased who was present during the last illness
- a relative of the deceased who was not present at the death or during the last illness but who lives in the district or sub-district where the death occurred
- a person who is not a relative but who was present at the time of death
- the occupier (e.g. the matron of a nursing home or warden of pensioners' flats) of the building where the death occurred, if he or she was aware of the details of the death
- any inmate of the building where the death occurred, if he or she was aware of the details of the death
- the person causing the disposal of the body (this means the person accepting the responsibility for arranging the funeral – *not* the funeral director, who is not allowed to register the death).

These categories of informants are given in order of precedence.

If the person has been found dead elsewhere, the following are qualified to register the death:

- any relative of the deceased able to provide the registrar with the required details
- any person present at the time of death
- the person who found the body
- the person in charge of the body (which will be the police if the body cannot be identified)
- the person accepting responsibility for arranging the funeral.

The responsibility for registering the death cannot be delegated to a person who is not qualified under the law to act as informant: should such a person attend the register office, the registrar will refuse to register the death and will require a qualified informant to attend. If the doctor is sending the medical certificate of cause of death direct to the registrar, sufficient time for the certificate to be delivered must be given before going to register the death.

If the registrar finds that the information the doctor has given on the medical certificate of cause of death is inadequate or that the death was due to some cause that should be reported to the coroner, he or she must inform the coroner accordingly and await written clearance before proceeding with the registration. He or she must also inform the coroner if it is found that the doctor had not seen the deceased within 14 days prior to death or after death. In cases where a coroner's inquest has been held, the coroner will act himself or herself as the informant and provide the registrar with all the necessary details; in this case there is no need for the family and relatives to register the death, although they will need to attend the register office if copies of the death certificate are needed.

Procedure

The procedure for registering a death is a simple question-and-answer interview between the registrar and the informant.

The registrar will, first of all, make sure that the death took place in his or her sub-district; a death cannot be registered if it occurred in any place outside the registrar's sub-district. He or she will ask in what capacity whoever is registering the death qualifies to be the informant – relative, present at the death, or other reason. The registrar may ask if the informant has brought the deceased's birth certificate and marriage certificate, and National Health Service medical card. It is not essential for the informant to have these, but they contain some of the information the registrar will need.

Then the registrar fills in a draft form for the register of deaths with the date of death and exactly where it occurred, the sex, names and surname of the dead person. It is as well to give all the names by which the deceased had ever been known, so that there can be no doubt who the particulars refer to. In order to avoid difficulties over identity in connection with probate, insurance policies, pensions and bank accounts, the names should be the same as those on birth and marriage certificates, and on any other relevant documents. The maiden surname of a married woman is required. The date and place of birth of the dead person, and last address are entered. For someone who died away from home, the home address should be given.

Next, the registrar will ask what was the last full-time occupation of the deceased, and whether he or she was retired at the time of death. A woman who was married or widowed at the time of her death would be described as 'wife of' or 'widow of', followed by the name and occupation of her husband, in addition to her own occupation or profession. A woman who had never been married or a woman whose marriage had been dissolved would have her occupation recorded, with no reference to her marital status.

Children under the age of 16 are described as 'son of' or 'daughter of', followed by the names and occupations of the parents.

The registrar copies the medical cause of death from the doctor's certificate or the coroner's notification, and adds the name and qualification of the doctor or coroner.

On the draft form, but not in the register itself, the registrar enters the deceased's National Health Service number. If the deceased was over 16 years old, additional information is requested: marital status at the time of death (single, married, widowed or divorced) and the date of birth of any widow or widower left. This information is not entered in the register in

England and Wales, and is used only for the preparation of population statistics by the Registrar General.

The registrar will ask for the deceased's medical card. This is to enable the National Health Service register to be kept up to date.

Entry in the register

Many register offices are now computerised; it is likely that your information about the deceased will be entered into a computer system and your copy, or copies, of the death certificate produced by a computer printer. Do not be surprised by this, but note that you will still be required to sign the register in the usual way.

The informant should check the draft of the proposed entry in the register to make sure that there is nothing wrong or misleading in it. When the particulars are agreed, the registrar makes the entry in the register itself and asks the informant to check and sign it. The informant should sign his or her usual signature, even if this is not his or her whole name. The registrar has to use special ink for the register, so sign with the pen offered.

After adding the date of the registration, the registrar signs the entry in the final space. Any errors can be corrected without formality before the entry has been signed, but once it is signed by the registrar, the entry cannot be corrected without the authority of the Registrar General, who may require documentary evidence to justify the correction. The registrar can now let you have copies of the entry in the register (the death certificates) which you may need for probate and other purposes.

Make a note of the number of the entry in the register and the date, and of the registration district, because you may need more copies of the entry later. Copies of entries in the current register cost £2.50, increasing to £5.50 after about one month, once the register is in the custody of the Superintendent Registrar.

Registering a stillbirth

The process of registering a stillbirth is a mixture of registering a birth and registering a death and has to be done within 42 days.

People qualified to register a stillbirth are (as for live births): the mother; the father if the child would have been legitimate had it been born alive; the occupier of the house or other premises in which the stillbirth occurred; a person who was present at the stillbirth or who found the stillborn child.

A stillborn child is a child born after the 24th week of pregnancy which did not at any time after being completely expelled from its mother breathe or show any other signs of life.

If a doctor was in attendance at a stillbirth or examined the body of the stillborn child, he or she can issue a certificate of stillbirth, stating the cause of stillbirth and the duration of the pregnancy. A certified midwife can also issue the certificate if no doctor was there. If no doctor or midwife was in attendance at, or after, the birth, one of the parents, or some other qualified informant, can make a declaration on a form (**Form 35**, available from the registrar of births and deaths), saying that to the best of his or her knowledge and belief the child was stillborn.

If there is any doubt whether the child was born alive or not, the case must be reported to the coroner of the district, who may then order a post mortem or an inquest and will issue a certificate of the cause of death when the inquiries are complete.

When registering a stillbirth, the registrar has to have the doctor's or midwife's certificate, or a declaration of the stillbirth. Whoever goes to register has to tell the registrar the name of the child where given, the name, surname and maiden name of the mother, her place of birth and her usual residence at the time of the child's birth; if she had never been married, her occupation is also required. If the child would have been legitimate, the name, surname and occupation of the father and his place of birth are required.

If the parents are not married at the time of their baby's birth but do still want the father's details entered, they should ask the registrar to guide them through the rather more involved procedures.

If the father and mother are married to each other, the registrar asks the month and year of the marriage, and the number of the mother's previous children, both born alive and stillborn, by her present and any former husband; this information is needed for statistical purposes only in order to forecast population trends and is not entered in the register.

DOCUMENTS FOR REGISTRATION

Notice to informant	from doctor	gives details of who must register death and what particulars will be required	via relative to registrar
Medical certificate of cause of death	from doctor	states cause of death	to registrar (direct or via relative)
If coroner involved: coroner's notification	from coroner	confirms or gives details of cause of death	to registrar (direct or via relative)
or			
Coroner's certificate after inquest	from coroner	gives all the particulars required for death to be registered	direct to registrar

No certified copy of the entry (death certificate) is given from the register of stillbirths unless the Registrar General's express permission has been obtained.

Expulsion of the foetus before the 24th week does not fall within the legal definition of a stillbirth and is usually considered a miscarriage. If the mother was in hospital at the time, the hospital may offer to arrange for the disposal of the remains. But if the parent(s) would like these to be buried or cremated in the usual way, it should be possible to arrange this with a local cemetery or crematorium, provided a form of medical certificate is completed.

Most crematoria make minimal charges for the funerals of stillborn or miscarried children and many funeral directors will provide their services on such occasions free of charge. This means that they will probably not charge for their professional services but will be obliged to pass on any fees for crematoria etc. that they may incur on behalf of their clients. Some hospitals now offer 'reverent disposal' of stillborn and miscarried children, which often involves a simple ceremony led by the hospital chaplain. It should be noted that in such cases there may be no ashes produced for subsequent burial or scattering. See also **Chapter 19**.

Chapter 3

DEATH IN HOSPITAL

THE CENTRE for Policy on Ageing produced a study in 1983 which found that 70 per cent of deaths in urban areas at that time took place in hospital: the percentage has since increased considerably. When someone has died in a hospital or similar institution, what happens up to the time of registration is slightly different from the way that arrangements are made if the death occurred at home.

The relatives, or whoever was named as next of kin when the patient was admitted, are informed of the death by the ward nursing staff. If death was unexpected, the result of an accident, or occurred during an operation or while the patient was recovering from an anaesthetic, the coroner will be involved. Normally, all deaths occurring within 24 hours of an operation will be reported to the coroner; when death occurs under suspicious circumstances, or is due to a medical mishap, industrial disease, violence, neglect, abortion, or any kind of poisoning, then the coroner must, by law, be informed. If the person who died was not already an in-patient at the hospital, a member of the family may be asked to identify the body.

Hospitals differ from each other in procedure, but it is usually the administrative rather than the medical staff who make the necessary arrangements with the relatives. In cases where the coroner is involved, it will not be possible to issue a medical certificate of the cause of death (see **Chapter 6**), but in normal cases this is usually completed by a hospital doctor and given to the next of kin. If the person concerned died before a hospital doctor had a chance to diagnose the cause, then the deceased patient's own doctor may sometimes be asked to issue the medical certificate. If the GP feels that there is reasonable doubt as to the cause of death, he or she will be unable to sign the certificate, and this too will be reported to the coroner. Once the coroner becomes involved, the responsibility for the body lies with the coroner's office and no longer with the hospital. The coroner, through his or her officer, will provide relatives with the necessary information; the hospital will tell the relatives how to contact the coroner's office.

All hospitals have considerable experience of dealing with bereaved relatives, and the staff appointed to this duty are usually patient and sympathetic. However, demands on time are considerable, emergencies often arise, and it is inevitable that, from time to time, some waiting will be involved. The hospital will make its procedures clear, but if death occurs in the evening or the middle of the night, an appointment will be made to deal with the formalities on the following day. The deceased's possessions will have to be removed from the hospital; these are normally available from the hospital's property office, and are only made available to the next of kin, or his or her authorised representative. A signature on a form of receipt will be required for any property removed.

If the medical certificate of the cause of death can be issued at the hospital, the relatives of the deceased have to arrange for the body to be removed from the hospital mortuary. This is normally the responsibility of the funeral director (but see **Chapter 14**). The hospital will not recommend any particular funeral director, but can provide a list of names and addresses of funeral directors in the local area. The funeral director concerned should be informed of the situation as soon as possible; most operate a 24-hour emergency service, but there is no need to inform him or her of a hospital death occurring in the middle of the night until next morning. The next of kin or executor will normally have to sign a form authorising the removal of the body to the funeral director's premises. If the funeral is to involve cremation, the necessary medical forms will be completed at the hospital; the body cannot be removed until this is done, and will sometimes involve a delay of up to 48 hours – longer if a weekend is included. There is a charge for these forms: this is usually paid by the funeral director, and the amount added to the funeral account.

Post mortem

Hospitals sometimes want to carry out a post mortem examination, or autopsy, to find out more about the cause of death. This 'hospital post mortem' does not involve the coroner and cannot be undertaken without the permission of the next of kin: the next of kin, or executor, should therefore be prepared to give a response to this question when visiting the hospital after death has occurred. In cases where the coroner *is* involved, permission for a post mortem is not required: should the coroner order a post mortem, the law requires that it must take place. Relatives will not automatically be told the results of a post mortem, and should ask for the results if they want to know. Under some circumstances, relatives may be asked if they have any objection to the use of the deceased's organs for transplant surgery. Even if the patient had completed a donor card, the relatives will be consulted before any organs are removed (see **Chapter 4**).

Registration

The procedure for registering a death is the same as for a death that occurred at home, but the registration must be done at the registrar's office in the registration district where the hospital is situated. However, if that same registration district or sub-district has another office, or out-station, which is nearer and therefore more convenient for the relatives, registration may be carried out there.

At the time of writing, February 1994, discussion had taken place on allowing information on the death to be given in a district other than where the death took place. However, until further notice deaths must be registered in the district or sub-district where death occurred, except in Scotland (see **Chapter 7**).

Funeral arrangements

Where there are no relatives or friends to arrange and meet the cost of the funeral, the health authority is empowered to do so.

Hospitals have arrangements with local funeral directors to provide a simple funeral. Although, technically, the health authority bears the responsibility, in practice, the funeral arrangements are made by the staff of the hospital where the patient died.

CHAPTER 4

ORGAN DONATION FOR TRANSPLANTATION

WHILE the number of transplants carried out in this country has increased dramatically, there are still long waiting lists. The most useful organs to be considered for transplantation are the kidneys, heart, heart and lung, lungs, liver, and the cornea of the eye. Many people now carry a donor card and hope that by making their body organs available their death might enable someone else to live. In fact, with the exception of the cornea, organs can only become useful for transplantation purposes if the deceased has died in hospital, where normal bodily functions can be maintained by use of a ventilator. In order for major organs to be suitable for transplantation, the person concerned must be under 70 years of age, have suffered complete and irreversible brain stem damage, be maintained on a ventilator and have no malignancy (other than a primary brain tumour). He or she must be free from major sepsis (pus-forming bacteria), be HIV-negative, and of a compatible blood group with the recipient.

Of course, the organs themselves must be healthy, and the donor patient in a reasonably healthy condition. Smoking, for instance, may make a potential donor's organs unusable.

Donor cards

The removal of organs for transplantation is permitted by law if the dead person had previously indicated willingness to become a donor, usually by signing a donor card. However, hospital staff will always consult the relatives about possible donation, and, if there is any objection, it is unlikely that the organs will be used. There is, however, no legal requirement to obtain permission from the donor's relatives before donation can take place, but the person in charge of the body must satisfy themselves that the donor's consent was not withdrawn after signing the card.

If there is no donor card, the hospital staff may ask the relatives if there is any objection to organ donation. Understandably, this thought may not be upper-most in the minds of the recently bereaved, but decisions must be made quickly if the organs are to be of any use. Wherever possible, potential organ donations should be discussed well before death occurs; many people are reluctant to do this, but a readiness to face the situation would bring life and hope to many.

Various hospitals have individual policies which depart from strict legal rights, and thus may give differing advice; the situation as above is the considered advice given by the Legal Services Department of the Royal College of Nursing.

Should the coroner be involved, his or her consent must always be gained before any organ donation takes place. Other than this, the process for organ donation should not delay the funeral arrangements, and the death can be registered in the normal way.

Corneal transplants

The corneas from the eyes of someone who has died can be used to restore sight. They are usually removed by taking the whole eye and, although best removed within six hours of death, can actually be usefully removed within 12–24 hours after death has occurred, whether at home or in hospital.

There is no upper age limit (although organs of children under two years of age cannot normally be used due to incomplete development), since corneal grafts often take place for elderly people, and an age match is preferred. The colour of the eyes and the sex, race, blood group and tissue type of the donor are irrelevant. With corneal transplants, there is no need for the donor to be maintained on a ventilator, and the need to wear glasses does not normally affect suitability. The eyes will be used as long as there is no relevant past medical history of eye surgery.

Until recently, only surgeons were allowed to remove donor eye tissue, so if a donor died at home or in a different hospital, a surgeon had to recover the valuable corneal tissue. The Corneal Transplant Act of 1986 now allows properly qualified technicians to remove corneal tissue – as there are more technicians than surgeons, a greater number of donated corneas can now be retrieved. Some 2,000 corneal transplants took place in 1987, of which 90 per cent were successful.

Relatives who want to carry out the wishes of the deceased in the case of corneal donation should first of all consult the donor's GP and/or the ophthalmic department of the local hospital. In all cases, action must be taken as quickly as possible. A special corneal transplant service (run by the Department of Health as part of the UK transplant service, with contributory funding from the Iris Fund for Prevention of Blindness*) takes corneas from donors to the nearest hospital grafting centre or eye bank with minimal delay.

Brain stem death

If the body of a potential donor were to be left until the traditional signs of death were apparent (lack of pulse, coldness, rigor mortis etc.) the organs would have deteriorated through lack of oxygen and no longer be of any use. Consequently, death now has to be determined through assessment of irreversible brain stem damage. Brain stem death occurs when the part of the brain responsible for maintaining the essential functions of the body is irreversibly damaged. In order to ascertain whether or not brain stem death has occurred, the cranial nerves are tested by a stringent and approved set of six tests in accordance with criteria laid down by the Conference of Royal Medical Colleges. The examination is carried out by a consultant, and repeated by another consultant or senior registrar who is clinically independent of the first. Neither will be a member of the transplant team. The official time of death is given as the point at which the second set of tests is completed.

BODY
BODY, the British Organ Donors Society, is a voluntary organisation, formed in 1984, whose objectives are to relieve sickness and protect health by promoting the carrying of donor cards. The society is a charitable trust, and acts as a help and support group for donor and recipient families. Those wanting further information should contact BODY*.

Body donated for medical education or research

A number of people express the wish that their body should be used after death for medical research. Bodies donated in this way are used by doctors and medical students who are studying and researching the structure and function of the normal human body. (Research into specific medical diseases is not carried out in these examinations.) If such a wish was expressed by the deceased, the next of kin or executor should immediately telephone HM Inspector of Anatomy* for details of the relevant anatomy school.

Medical schools are, in fact, offered far more bodies than can possibly be accepted and it should be recognised that the offering or willing of a body to medical research does not necessarily mean that it will be accepted. Or, at the time of death there may be some specific reason why the body cannot be accepted: for instance, if the coroner is involved, if death has occurred as the result of certain illnesses, or if death occurs too far away for the relevant medical school to transport the body practically. Until acceptance of the body is confirmed, the family should continue to make arrangements for the funeral in case the body is not accepted.

Arrangements prior to death

If a body is to be accepted for medical research, it is imperative that arrangements are made with a specific medical school well before death occurs; specific forms must be completed in advance and should be left with the family, bank or solicitor along with instructions for immediate action when death occurs. If the body is accepted, arrangements will be made by the medical school for it to be collected straight away by a contracted funeral director and taken to the school. In the meantime, the next of kin or executor should obtain the medical certificate of the cause of death from the doctor in charge of the case and register the death as soon as possible. The green Registrar's Certificate for burial or cremation should also be sent to the medical school.

Funeral arrangements

It is the responsibility of the medical school to arrange and pay for burial or cremation when the appropriate time comes. The family and executors need make no further arrangements: burial or cremation will be provided according to the wishes of the deceased and next of kin. If the body is eventually to be cremated, the executor may be asked to complete and sign the statutory application form for cremation, **Form A**; however, this may also be signed by the professor of the medical school.

The medical school will pay all expenses for a simple funeral, unless the relatives ask to be allowed to make their own arrangements, at which point the body will be given back and the funeral expenses will become the responsibility of the family. If the medical school makes the funeral arrangements, a simple ceremony will be conducted by a minister or priest of the faith professed by the deceased, unless otherwise requested. The medical school does not put up individual headstones.

If the relatives of the deceased do not wish to make funeral arrangements themselves, but ask for burial or cremation in some place other than that normally used by the medical school, or if they request more elaborate arrangements than those normally provided, the extra expense must be met by the family. Some medical schools give no option on the method or procedure of funerals they arrange.

CHAPTER 5

AFTER REGISTRATION

IN ORDER to make certain necessary arrangements regarding the deceased's legal and financial affairs, one or more death certificates may be needed. These are not the same as the medical certificate of cause of death signed by a doctor at the time of death, but are certified copies of the entry in the Register of Deaths (the 'standard' death certificate). One certificate each will be needed to apply for probate or letters of administration (see **Chapter 20**), for dealing with the deceased's bank account and for claims on insurance policies. Each will cost £2.50 if obtained at the time of registration or within a few weeks afterwards.

If advice is needed about the number and type of certificates required, a list of the purposes for which evidence of death may be required should be taken to the registrar, who will advise accordingly.

Notifying the DSS

The DSS must be informed about the death in order to deal with pensions etc.; the registrar will provide a free form for this purpose – this form (**344/BD8**) should also be used to claim various Social Security benefits after someone has died, but it cannot be used to apply to the Social Fund for help with the cost of the funeral. For this, a different form (**SF200**) is needed, which can be obtained from the local Social Security office. The funeral director who is dealing with the funeral arrangements may also keep copies, and will assist with completing them and submitting them to the local DSS.

There is no longer any form of general death grant; this was abolished some years ago.

Registrar's certificate for burial or cremation

Together with copies of the death certificate and Social Security Form 344/BD8, the registrar will provide a green certificate to say that the death has been registered and that a funeral may take place. Before issuing this certificate, the registrar must have a properly completed medical certificate of the cause of death signed by a doctor. This green certificate permits burial or cremation to take place and must be given to the funeral director: the funeral cannot take place without it. If the coroner is involved, a different legal process is involved (see **Chapter 6**).

If the informant is unable to attend the registrar's office within the five days required for notification, the registrar, provided he or she has received a medical certificate of cause of death from the doctor, may issue a certificate for burial, but *not* for cremation.

Careful examination of the registrar's certificate will show whether it has been issued before or after registration: if it states that it was issued *before* registration, it is suitable for burial only, but if issued *after* registration it is suitable for burial or cremation.

The funeral director will send this registrar's certificate either to the cemetery authority or vicar of the churchyard where burial is to take place, or to the office of the local crematorium in the case of cremation.

Obtaining death certificates at a later date

Further copies of death certificates may be obtained from the registrar who registered the death while the current volume of the death register remains in use. This is likely to be about one month, but the time varies according to how many deaths are registered each week and whether the death in question was entered near the beginning or end of the relevant register.

When completed, each death register is passed to the Superintendent Registrar of the district, from whom copies of the death certificate can be obtained later if required. The charge for each certificate in this case is £5.50.

If the death was registered more than two years previously, applications for certificates by post can be made to the General Register Office★. The charge for this service is £15. With any postal application, a stamped, addressed envelope should be sent, together with a cheque or postal order for the necessary amount. When applying in person to the registrar for a copy of the certificate, payment must be made at the time of application.

Northern Ireland
In Northern Ireland, contact the Registrar General (Northern Ireland)★. The charge for a standard death certificate at a later date is also £5.50, which includes the search fee. (For details regarding registration and obtaining death certificates in Scotland, see **Chapter 7**).

CHAPTER 6

THE CORONER

THE OFFICE of the coroner is ancient: it originated in Saxon times and received a new emphasis in Norman times, when the king wanted money to pursue his holy wars. The full title was *Coronae Curia Regis* (Keeper of the Royal Pleas) and the coroner was responsible for investigating accidents such as shipwrecks – mainly to see what money could be gained for the crown thereby – and the evaluation of treasure trove. He became responsible for keeping a record of all sudden, unexpected deaths – currently, the subject of most of the coroner's work.

The modern coroner is a qualified doctor or solicitor who is paid by the local authority, but remains independent of both local and central government, being responsible only to the Crown. He or she is assisted by the coroner's officer, usually a police officer; it is the coroner's officer who is generally in contact with the public.

Deaths to be reported to the coroner

When a death occurs which may not be due to natural causes, it must be reported to the coroner. Even if it is fairly evident that death is due to natural causes, but the deceased had not been seen by a doctor for 14 days prior to death, or had not been seen at all by a doctor before or after death, the coroner must be informed. The coroner will then consult with the deceased's GP, who will usually be able to advise whether he or she is satisfied as to the cause of death; the coroner will then cease to be involved and will issue the certificate; the family will then register the death as normal. The doctor is not legally allowed to sign the death certificate if he or she had not seen the patient within this period, even if he or she is confident about the cause of death: the coroner must be consulted. In Northern Ireland, the relevant period is 28 days.

In any case where the doctor is at all uncertain as to the cause of death, the death must be reported to the coroner. Any death attributable to industrial disease, or where compensation has been claimed because of this, must be reported to the coroner (see page 38); in some cases, death caused or accelerated by injury received during military service, however long ago, must also be reported.

Other circumstances in which a death must be reported to the coroner include when death:

- was sudden and unexplained
- occurred in suspicious circumstances
- was caused directly or indirectly by any kind of accident
- might have been due to neglect, any kind of poisoning, dependence on or abuse of drugs, or abortion
- was suicide
- occurred while in prison or in police custody
- took place during a surgical operation or before recovery from the effects of anaesthesia.

Reporting the death

Anyone who is uneasy about the apparent cause of a death has the right to inform the coroner for the district. By telephoning a police station, you can find out who is the relevant coroner and how to get in touch with him or her. Or you can give information to any local police station, who will pass the information to the coroner's officer.

The information does not have to be an allegation of some crime. There may be some circumstances which you feel are contributory to the death but may not have been known to the doctor – such as an old war wound or injury – which can be established by a post mortem examination. If you believe that the deceased may have died from some industrial disease, it is obviously best to inform the coroner before the person is cremated, otherwise the matter can never be resolved.

Generally, however, it is the doctor who reports a death to the coroner, or the police. Medical certificates of the cause of death carry a list of the type of cases that the doctor should report to the coroner. If the death comes within any of these categories, the usual practice is for the doctor to inform the coroner directly, before anyone has gone to register the death.

It may be that the registrar, when he or she gets the doctor's medical certificate of the cause of death, decides that because of the cause or circumstances of the death, he or she must report the death to the coroner. In such cases, there will be a delay before the death can be registered, which may interfere with the arrangements that the family had hoped to make for the funeral.

The coroner may decide that there is no need for further investigation, being satisfied that the cause of death is known to be natural, and that the death can be registered from the certificate provided by the doctor. In this case, the coroner sends a formal notice of the decision to the registrar of the district, and the death can then be registered in the usual way by the qualified informant.

If the registrar knows who the next of kin are, he or she gets in touch with them and tells them that he or she is now in a position to register the death. If the death had been reported to the coroner direct and the registrar does not know who the next of kin are, they will have to find out from the coroner's office when to go to the registrar.

Coroner's investigations

When a death is reported to the coroner and he or she decides to investigate, that death cannot be registered until the coroner provides a certificate when inquiries are complete. He or she will usually order a post mortem, which will often show that death was due to natural causes; in this case, he or she will notify the family and the registrar through the coroner's officer, and the death can then be registered in the normal way. If the funeral is to involve burial, the registrar will issue a certificate for burial. If it is to involve cremation, it is the coroner who will issue a coroner's **Form E** for cremation; one part (pink) will be given to the family or sent direct to the registrar, while the other part (yellow) will be sent to the funeral director, or direct to the crematorium.

The actual funeral will have to wait for the outcome of the coroner's investigations, but in many cases the coroner's officer will be able to give a reasonably accurate indication of how long these will take. The funeral director involved will normally consult with the coroner's officer, and will be able to make tentative funeral arrangements while the investigation is proceeding: it is not necessary to wait until the investigation ends before beginning to make arrangements.

In many cases, the coroner's involvement is a formality, and reporting a death to the coroner does not inevitably mean a post mortem or an inquest. The coroner concerned will decide what action must be taken.

Post mortem

The majority of post mortem examinations are ordered by the coroner to establish the cause of death. This may be to show that the death was a natural one or it may resolve a dispute where the family might believe that the death was caused by an industrial disease (a person may have suffered from an industrial illness in life but die from some other, unrelated, cause). In a few cases, the post mortem provides valuable evidence of the manner of a criminal death.

The coroner orders a post mortem if the law requires this. The family of the deceased do not have to be asked to give their consent, as they would be when a hospital wants to perform a post mortem examination. The coroner arranges and pays for the post mortem.

If members of the family object to a post mortem examination for religious or other reasons, or if they have any reason to believe that the examination is not necessary, they should inform the coroner. If the coroner is still of the opinion that the examination is required, the family can apply to the High Court to reverse the decision of the coroner. This will delay arrangements for the disposal of the body.

If the post mortem reveals that the death was due to natural causes and no other circumstance warrants further investigation, the coroner notifies the registrar and the death can be registered in the usual way. In some districts, the coroner's officer or another police officer calls on the family to tell them; otherwise, the next of kin should enquire at the coroner's office every few days to find out when the coroner's notification is being sent to the registrar. The coroner has no duty to inform the next of kin of the result of the post mortem.

After the post mortem, the body again becomes the responsibility of the family. To avoid unnecessary delays, the family can arrange for a funeral director to collect the necessary forms from the coroner's office as soon as these are available and make arrangements for the funeral at the earliest suitable date.

Inquest

The coroner is obliged to hold an inquest into every violent and unnatural death that is reported, and also following the death of a person in prison.

An inquest is an inquiry to determine who the deceased person was, and how, when and where that person died, and to establish the particulars that are required for the registration of the death.

An inquest is held formally and is open to the public. A person wishing to attend, but who has not been given notice of the inquest, can ask at a local police station or telephone the coroner's office to find out when the inquest is being held. The coroner may have asked for further investigations and tests to be carried out, and the date for the inquest will not be arranged until these are all complete.

Adjournments

Coroners are increasingly prepared to open an inquest and then adjourn it 'to a date to be fixed' or for a specific number of days. While police time is not always instantly available, this enables routine enquiries to be completed without holding up burial or cremation arrangements. If it is clear to the coroner that disposal of the body will not prejudice such enquiries, he or she can take evidence of identification and of the cause of death and may then adjourn the inquest, often for a short period, until inquiries are complete – issuing the necessary order for burial or the cremation certificate before the adjournment.

Adjournments also have to be made to allow extra time in more complex matters – to await the result, for example, of an inquiry into an air crash or other disaster. The coroner may provide any properly introduced person with an interim certificate of the fact of death. This will allow insurance or other payments to be claimed and the estate to be administered.

An inquest must be adjourned where a person has been charged with causing the death or with an offence connected with it that will be the subject of a trial before a Crown Court jury. The coroner will then send notification to the registrar for the registration of the death.

At the court

The coroner's court is a court of law with power to summon witnesses and jurors, and with power to deal with any contempt in the face of the court.

The law requires that any person with evidence to give concerning the death should attend an inquest. In practice, the coroner will have read any written statements that have been made, and will know the names of those who have been interviewed by the police and by the coroner's officers. The witnesses the coroner knows will be needed are summoned to the inquest. The summons is often an informal telephone call but there may be a written summons or a subpoena (if the witness is outside the jurisdiction of the coroner). A witness is entitled to travel expenses and to a fixed sum to compensate for loss of earnings.

If any witnesses know that they cannot attend, they should inform the coroner's office at once. When a witness has been formally summoned, there are penalties for failing to attend. Non-attendance causes inconvenience, and expense to the family if the inquest has to be adjourned.

Unlike a trial, there are no 'sides' at an inquest. Anyone who is regarded as having a proper interest may ask witnesses questions at an inquest and may be legally represented. The list of people with a 'proper interest' includes parents, children and spouse of the deceased, insurers and beneficiaries of an insurance policy on the life of the deceased, any person whose conduct is called into question regarding the cause of the death, and, in appropriate cases, a chief officer of police, government inspector or trade union official.

There is a minimum amount of pomp and ceremony at an inquest. The coroner calls witnesses in turn from the main part of the court to come up to the witness box. Eash witness swears or affirms to 'speak the truth, the whole truth and nothing but the truth'.

First, the coroner questions the witness; then, with his or her permission, the witness can be examined by anyone present who has a proper interest in the case (or by that person's legal representative). If you know that you will want to give evidence or examine a witness, tell the coroner's officer beforehand, so that the coroner can call you at the right moment. When all the witnesses have been heard, the coroner sums up (there are no speeches by the lawyers) and gives the verdict.

With a jury

Some inquests have to be heard before a jury. The jury is summoned in the same way as a crown court jury. In cases of industrial accidents or other incidents that must be reported to a government department, after a death in prison or in police custody or caused by the act of a police officer, and where death was in circumstances that present a danger to the public, there is always a jury.

The jury for an inquest consists of not fewer than seven and not more than 11 men or women eligible for jury service. There is not the power to challenge jurors – there is no accused person to exercise the power. The jurors are on oath. Jurors need not view the body unless the coroner directs them to.

At the conclusion of his or her inquiries, the coroner sums up the evidence to the jury and explains the law. All the findings of the inquest are then made by the jury. Jurors do not usually leave the court to discuss their decision but may do so. They can return a majority verdict.

The verdict

The purpose of an inquest is not only to find out who the deceased person was and how, when and where he or she came by his or her death, but also to decide the category of death. This is colloquially called the verdict but the correct description is the conclusion. It can range from natural causes to suicide, industrial disease or unlawful killing. Conclusions are subject to many legal technicalities. In particular, the finding of suicide must be strictly proved: when there is no conclusive evidence of the intent to commit suicide, the coroner has to return an open verdict.

The conclusion must not appear to determine any matter of criminal liability against a named person, nor any matter of civil liability.

A verdict of accidental death does not mean that there will be no prosecution in a magistrates' court or that the family cannot bring an action for damages. All it means is that it is not a case of suicide or homicide. The 'properly interested persons' are entitled to a copy of the notes of the evidence and these are often useful in subsequent proceedings.

The press and inquests

Since inquests are held in public, the press can be present. There are restrictions on the publication of the names of minors, but in other matters there are no reporting restrictions.

Death is always a sensational subject. Although the coroner may try to choose words carefully, people giving evidence or questioning witnesses may provide comments that can be distressing to the family. The coroner will try to ensure that the facts are as accurate as possible; the inquest may be able to dispel rumours and inaccurate assertions.

The cost

There should be no expense to the family arising out of an inquest. Representation by a lawyer is not necessary in the majority of inquests, and in cases where there is no controversy, the family should not make an unnecessary expenditure at such a time. There is no provision for representation at an inquest under the legal aid scheme.

Many people think it wise, however, to be represented by a solicitor at the inquest in the case of death resulting from an accident or an occupational disease, because there may be compensation claims to be made later and a solicitor would be better able to make use of the evidence presented at an inquest.

Someone who does not know of a solicitor can go to a Citizens Advice Bureau, which can arrange a free or small-fee interview with a lawyer. The CAB will ensure that a family that has just lost the person providing their income does not pay out money unnecessarily, and may also advise on any prospect of some compensation.

After the inquest
In all cases other than those where someone has been charged with a serious offence, the coroner would already have sent the certificate after adjournment, but registration of the death usually takes place when the coroner sends a certificate after inquest to the registrar of births and deaths of the district in which the death took place or in which the body was found. This certificate provides the registrar with the information needed to register the death. No informant is required to attend the registrar's office. The death certificates can be obtained by the family from the registrar any time after the inquest.

Certificate for burial or cremation

Once a death has been registered, the registrar issues a green certificate, referred to generally as the disposal certificate, authorising either burial or application for cremation. A body cannot be buried or cremated without this certificate or its equivalent – namely, the coroner's order for burial or certificate for cremation. It is unwise to make more than provisional arrangements for the funeral until you have the certificate from the registrar or the coroner. You will get a burial or cremation certificate from the registrar or from the coroner but not from both.

The registrar can issue a certificate before registering a death but only when he or she has already received the requisite information (including medical evidence) and is just waiting for the informant to come to register the death. This may arise, for instance, when the only suitable informant is ill in hospital but the funeral has to take place. A certificate issued by the registrar before registration authorises burial only; crematorium authorities are not allowed to accept such a certificate.

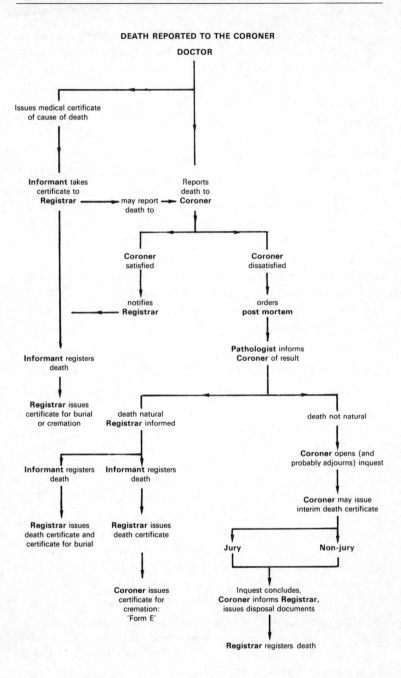

DEATH REPORTED TO THE CORONER

If the death has been reported to the coroner and a post mortem examination has been ordered, only the coroner can authorise cremation; if the body is to be buried, the registrar can issue the burial certificate. If there has been an inquest, it is the coroner who issues either an order for burial or a certificate for cremation.

No fee is charged for a registrar's certificate or coroner's order. If you lose it, you (or the funeral director) have to apply to the registrar or the coroner who issued the original certificate for a duplicate.

Once you have obtained the necessary certificate from the registrar or the coroner, give it to the funeral director who will take it to the church, cemetery or crematorium officials. Without it, they will not bury or cremate a body. It is the responsibility of the church, cemetery or crematorium to complete **Part C** of the certificate and to return it to the registrar confirming disposal has taken place. If the registrar does not receive Part C within 14 days of the issue of the certificate, he or she will get in touch with the person to whom the certificate had been given to find out what is happening.

CHAPTER 7

PROCEDURES IN SCOTLAND

THE MEDICAL *certificate of the cause of death given by doctors in Scotland is similar to that in England. The obligation to give the certificate rests on the doctor who attended the deceased during the last illness but, if there was no doctor in attendance, the certificate may be issued by any doctor who is able to do so. The doctor hands the certificate to a relative to take to the local registrar or sends it direct to the registrar. In the majority of cases, the certificate is issued to a relative.*

If a medical certificate of cause of death cannot be given, the registrar can, nevertheless, register the death but must report the facts of the case to the procurator fiscal.

The procurator fiscal

There are no coroners in Scotland and the duties which in England would be carried out by a coroner are in Scotland carried out by a procurator fiscal. The procurator fiscal is a full-time law officer, who comes under the authority of the Lord Advocate.

The procurator fiscal has many functions, including responsibility for investigating all unexpected and violent deaths and also any death which occurred under suspicious circumstances. If satisfied with the doctor's medical certificate and any evidence received from the police, he or she need take no further action. If, however, the procurator fiscal considers a further medical report is necessary, a medical practitioner will be requested (frequently a police surgeon) to report 'on soul and conscience' what he or she considers was the cause of death.

Post mortem
In the majority of cases, a post mortem is not carried out and the doctor certifies the cause of death after an external examination. The mere fact

that the cause of death is in a medical sense unexplained is not a ground for ordering a dissection at public expense, provided the intrinsic circumstances explain sufficiently the cause of death in a popular sense and do not raise a suspicion of criminality or negligence.

In cases where the procurator fiscal decides a post mortem is necessary, permission to carry it out is given by the sheriff. One doctor is usually sufficient but if, while conducting the dissection, the doctor finds unexpected difficulties, the procurator fiscal may decide to bring in a second doctor. Where there is a possibility of criminal proceedings being taken against someone and it is necessary to prove the fact and cause of death, a post mortem should be carried out by two medical practitioners.

Public inquiry

Death while in legal custody or as the result of an accident during work must be the subject of a public inquiry (called a Fatal Accident Inquiry or FAI), which takes the place of an inquest in England. If a person, while engaged in industrial employment or occupation, died of natural causes, there may, but will not necessarily, be a public inquiry.

The procurator fiscal has to report certain cases to the Crown Office and it is the Lord Advocate who makes the final decision about whether to apply to a sheriff for an inquiry to be held. In all other cases, investigations made into sudden deaths are carried out by the procurator fiscal confidentially.

Before reporting a case to the Crown Office, the procurator fiscal interviews witnesses and the relatives in private (this is called a precognition).

Cases which are reported to the Crown Office because they may result in a public inquiry are essentially those involving a matter of the public interest – for instance, to prevent a recurrence of similar circumstances. Deaths which are directly or indirectly connected with the action of a third party, such as road traffic deaths, may be reported to the Crown Office for consideration either of criminal proceedings or of a public inquiry.

A public inquiry is heard before the sheriff in the local sheriff court. The procurator fiscal examines the witnesses but it is the sheriff who determines the circumstances of the death.

When the inquiry is completed, the procurator fiscal notifies the result of the findings to the Registrar General. If the death has already been registered, the Registrar General lets the local registrar know if any changes need to be made to the entry. If the death has not already been registered, the Registrar General instructs the registrar of the district in which the death occurred to register the death.

Registering the death

In Scotland the law requires that every death must be registered within eight days from the date of death.

The person qualified to act as informant for registering a death is any relative of the deceased, any person present at the death, the deceased's executor or other legal representative, the occupier of the premises where the death took place, or any person having knowledge of the particulars to be registered.

Whereas in England a death must be registered in the registration office for the district in which the death occurred, in Scotland the death may be registered either in the office for the district in which the death occurred or in the office for the district in which the deceased had normally resided before the death, provided this was also in Scotland. The death of a visitor to Scotland must be registered where the death took place.

As in England, the procedure for registering a death is a simple question-and-answer interview between registrar and informant. The registrar will request the production of a medical certificate of cause of death or, failing that, the name and address of a doctor who can be asked to give the certificate. The information required by a Scottish registrar to register a death is much the same as in England and Wales, except that he or she also needs to know the time of death; if the deceased had ever been married, the name, surname and occupation of each spouse; the name and occupation of the deceased's father and the name and maiden surname of the mother, and whether the parents are alive or dead.

When the form of particulars has been completed, the registrar asks the informant to read it over carefully to ensure that all the particulars are correct, and to sign it. The registrar then makes the entry in the register and asks the informant to check it carefully and sign the entry before adding the date and his or her own signature.

Registering a stillbirth

A stillbirth in Scotland must be registered within 21 days. As in England, if no doctor or midwife can issue a certificate of stillbirth, an informant must make a declaration on a special form. In Scotland this is **Form 7**, obtainable from the registrar. All such cases, and any case where there is doubt as to whether the child was alive or not, are reported to the procurator fiscal, who notifies the Registrar General of the results of his or her investigations.

If the body is to be cremated, a certificate of stillbirth must be given by the doctor who was in attendance at the confinement (or who conducted a post mortem). The stillbirth must have been registered before cremation can take place.

A stillbirth can be registered either in the district in which it took place or in the district in Scotland in which the mother of the stillborn child was ordinarily resident at the time of the stillbirth.

The informant must produce for the registrar a doctor's or midwife's certificate, or the completed Form 7, and is required to give the same information as in England and, in addition, the time of the stillbirth and, where applicable, the place of the parents' marriage.

Certificate of registration

There is no direct equivalent in Scotland of a disposal certificate. After registration, the registrar issues to the informant a certificate of registration of death, which should be given to the funeral director to give to the keeper of the burial ground or to the crematorium authorities. There is no charge for this certificate.

Death certificates

As in England, the registrar issues, free of charge, a certificate of registration of death which can be used for National Insurance purposes only. All other death certificates must be paid for.

The full copy of an entry in the death register (the standard death certificate) costs £6 if applied for within one month of the date of registration. If applied for at a later date, the charge is £8.50. Each further copy of the same entry ordered at the same time costs £6. A special certificate, costing £5.50, is used for DSS claims.

Death certificates are always obtainable from the registrar of the district where the death was registered; they are also obtainable from the General Register Office (Scotland)★ at any time after about a year to 18 months from the date of registration. The same fees are charged if the application is made personally, but the fee is £10.50 if the application is made by post.

CHAPTER 8

DECISIONS ABOUT THE FUNERAL

WHEN SOMEONE dies, a number of decisions about the funeral have to be made fairly quickly. This is often a time of considerable emotional turmoil, so great care needs to be taken to make the right decisions. Many people want to 'get the funeral over with as soon as possible'; it is wise, however, to allow enough time to recover from the initial shock of the first 48 hours, and plan a funeral which will be an appropriate memorial to the person who has died.

If the deceased left no specific instructions, the decision about burial or cremation is normally made by the next of kin, or the executor. Although it is usual to carry out the wishes previously expressed by the deceased, there is no legal obligation to do so. Should it prove impossible to trace a living relative or friend willing to act as executor, the hospital or local authority will accept the responsibility of providing a minimum price funeral.

Whether the funeral is to involve burial or cremation, many of the arrangements can be made by a reasonably capable individual who knows what to do. However, most people feel the need of professional help at this time, and it is still rare for a funeral to be carried out without the services of a funeral director.

Funeral directors

William Russell, the first undertaker in the UK, began business in London in 1680, and was succeeded by carpenters who specialised in producing coffins, and carriage proprietors who developed special funeral carriages. These functions merged, and a profession of men who 'undertook' to provide a funeral service arose. The Victorian era saw the popularisation of elaborate, often ostentatious, and usually expensive funerals.

Undertakers are now known as funeral directors. The National Association of Funeral Directors★ consults with the government through the Office of Fair Trading. The NAFD insists that its members adhere to a carefully drawn up Code of Practice, which includes giving full information about services and prices, providing a written estimate of all charges and a detailed funeral account. Members must offer a basic funeral if requested to do so. The code covers general and professional conduct, including confidentiality and a procedure for complaints. Other professional groupings of funeral directors have come into being. The Funeral Standards Council (FSC) was formed in the summer of 1993, when the Co-operative Funeral Services withdrew their membership of the NAFD, complaining that the Code of Practice was not being adhered to. The FSC consists mainly of the various Co-operative Funeral Services. Since then other changes have occurred and other groups formed. At the time of writing (February 1994), the Office of Fair Trading deals only with the NAFD, although this may change in the forseeable future.

The funeral director's purpose is to assume total responsibility for organising and supplying all that is needed for a funeral, and to provide as much care as possible for the relatives. Increasingly, funeral directors offer bereavement care services, with qualified counsellors on the staff. Nevertheless, the arrangement of a funeral is a business transaction and should be treated as such; it is often difficult for bereaved relatives to be businesslike in the circumstances, but most funeral directors are understanding and will give all the assistance needed.

The family should agree who is to be in charge and supervise the arrangements; it is not part of an executor's formal duty to arrange the funeral, although it is a responsibility often taken on.

The cost of the funeral

At the time of arranging the funeral, you should have a fairly clear idea of the kind of funeral that is wanted, and approximately how much money should be spent on it. The funeral director can provide quotes for anything from a basic funeral to an elaborate arrangement costing a great deal of money.

Some people, during their lifetime, take out insurance to pay for their funeral, or join one of the friendly societies which pays out a lump sum on death. Pre-paid funeral plans are becoming increasingly popular: individuals choose the kind of funeral they would prefer and pay for it in advance at a slightly reduced rate (see also **Chapter 22**). The proceeds are then invested in a trust fund, which pays for all funeral expenses – however they may have increased – at the time of death. Some people find the expenses very difficult to meet and are embarrassed about telling the funeral director. In fact, one of the first things a funeral director should do is find out if there is a problem about money and, if so, whether he or she can help by applying for a grant from the DSS. Normally, the cost of the funeral is paid for from the deceased's estate – the money and property left.

If you require only the most basic kind of funeral, tell the funeral director at the outset; he or she will then tell you what can be provided and how much it will cost. Most funeral directors will not try to sell you something you do not want, but they are businessmen, and will make you aware of all the various services that can be offered, including providing flowers for the funeral and placing obituary notices in the local and national press.

You can make preliminary arrangements with a funeral director on the telephone, but to make full arrangements for the funeral it will be necessary either for him or her to come to your home, or for you to visit the office. There are papers to be signed and, in the case of cremation, legal documents. The funeral director should show you the price list for the funerals he or she can provide. You can ask for this in advance on the phone, and discuss the alternatives with the family. The funeral account will consist of two parts; first, the fees that the funeral director will pay out on your behalf – doctor's fees for cremation papers, crematorium fees, fees for the minister and organist, burial fees, grave digger, obituary, flowers etc. And second, the fees for professional services rendered – removal of the body, preparation and arrangements, use of the chapel of rest, coffin, hearse and limousine, funeral director and bearers etc. He or she will arrange, if asked, for orders of service to be printed and catering; for most of the disbursements the funeral director will pay in advance, and add the relevant amounts to the funeral account.

The lowest price for a basic funeral starts at not much less than £600 (1994 prices). This will vary according to which part of the country you live in, and will not include disbursements – about £230–50 for cremation, and often a great deal more for burial. For a basic funeral the funeral director will supply a hearse (but not a limousine), a simple coffin and funeral gown, use of the chapel of rest, and the services of a funeral director and four bearers for the funeral cortege, and will conduct all the necessary arrangements and preparation of the body. Many funeral directors will go well beyond the minimum requirements in supplying a basic funeral.

The funeral director will usually quote you an inclusive fee for his or her services according to the funeral you choose; if special services are required, such as several limousines or a casket for subsequent burial of cremated remains, these will incur extra charges. Many funeral directors make no charge at all for funerals of babies and small children, only passing on disbursement fees that may or may not be charged by churches or crematoria.

Burial or cremation

The choice of cremation may involve many different factors, but as far as cost is concerned, cremation is cheaper. Charges vary around the country, but an average cost of about £130 for cremation must be set against an average minimum cost of £350–£400 for burial in a municipal cemetery. Burial in a churchyard is considerably cheaper, about £150, but most churchyards have room only for the burial of ashes caskets. In the central areas of large cities, burial fees will increase to many hundreds – sometimes thousands – of pounds. The fees for the services of ministers are fixed annually by the Church of England, and followed by most other denominations; these and the fees for organists etc. will be the same for burial as for cremation.

Coffins

The price quoted for a complete funeral is based partly on the type of coffin requested, but will also involve other factors. If you choose one of the more expensive coffins, you will get a more elaborate standard of funeral. Different firms include different items in their inclusive charges; some charge extra for mourners' limousines, a car for the minister and for viewing the deceased during evenings or at weekends, while others would include these and other items within the basic fee. A funeral director should be able to show clients examples or illustrations of the different coffins and caskets he or she can supply.

The material from which a coffin is made greatly affects the price: the most basic type of coffin will be made from chipboard laminated with plastic foil; a standard type from veneered chipboard (similar to most modern furniture); and a superior coffin or casket from solid wood – such as tulip wood or oak. A casket is a more expensive form of coffin, rectangular in shape instead of the traditional tapered shape.

There is little variation in the cost of coffin linings and fittings, although if solid brass handles are requested, these will be expensive. For cremation, metal fittings are inadmissible; handles and fittings are made of plastic which has been electroplated with brass or nickel. Indeed, there are rigid by-laws which control the materials used in the construction of coffins for cremation; for each cremation, the funeral director must sign that he or she has conformed to the government's and crematorium's requirements.

Some funeral directors buy plain coffins, which are then lined and fitted with handles according to their client's choice; others buy them fitted and lined, and offer a variety of fitted coffins to their clients.

Each coffin must be fitted with a nameplate which contains the name of the deceased; it is normal for the plate also to contain the date of death and the deceased's age. It is worth remembering that the coffins offered for simple, basic funerals are intended for cremation rather than burial. In order to keep costs and prices down, the coffin is constructed to be suitable for carrying into a crematorium and placing on the catafalque: it may well not be sturdy enough to withstand the rigours of being lowered into a grave. It is advisable to choose a more sturdily constructed coffin if burial is envisaged; this does *not* mean buying the most expensive coffin – the funeral director will advise accordingly.

Other costs

It must be remembered that the total cost of the funeral will consist of the fees the funeral director will charge for his or her professional services, the fees paid to other agencies on behalf of the client, and any special services that are required beyond those supplied in the standard funeral package (such things as the removal of a body from a house or nursing home out of standard working hours, additional limousines, and a charge for mileage if the funeral involves travelling some considerable distance). There will also be an extra charge if the body is to be taken into church on the evening before the funeral, or for supplying a casket for the burial of cremated remains (ashes).

The funeral director should give an itemised written estimate of costs and a formal confirmation of funeral arrangements. Some clients feel that they do not want to be involved in too many practical decisions about the funeral, and want to leave it to the funeral director; a written estimate of the likely cost should still be provided. The estimate may well be amended as the bereaved relatives discuss the developing funeral arrangements, and decide on changes, such as the placement of obituaries, or an extra limousine. The estimate is a clear outline of what the funeral is likely to cost, but is *not* the bill: the funeral director will submit the account shortly after the funeral takes place.

Funeral directors will explain the charges and conditions made for different churches in the local area, and the differing fees charged by cemeteries and crematoria. Fees charged for burial in local municipal cemeteries may vary enormously within a short geographical distance, but it is common for local authorities to charge double or treble fees for burials of those who lived outside the local district. Fees for Anglican churches are fixed annually by the church authorities, and normally increase each year. At the time of writing (February 1994), the fees for a funeral service in an Anglian church were £43 for the service and £70 for burial in the churchyard after such a service. Fees for burial in a municipal cemetery will be very much more than this. Local churches often charge extra for the services of a verger, for heating and, sometimes, for use of the organ.

Nonconformist churches usually accept the same fees as those laid down for the Church of England, but frequently waive all charges when the burial is that of a member of the appropriate congregation.

Generally, the total cost of a funeral, including cremation, is unlikely to come to less than £900 (1994); burial will cost more – probably a lot more. Price levels, especially for burial, vary enormously between different parts of the country (especially in London, but also in other large cities); prices also vary between local funeral directors.

Help with funeral costs

Anyone on a low income will probably have great difficulty in meeting funeral costs, but may well be able to obtain help from the DSS Social Fund. There are rigid criteria for gaining assistance: the applicant must be receiving either Income Support, Family Credit, Housing Benefit, or Disability Working Allowance. This applies *only* to the person who is arranging the funeral: unfortunately, it makes no difference whether the person who died was receiving these benefits. Payments are made from the Social Fund to eligible applicants, and have to be paid back out of the estate of the deceased if money becomes available. Funeral directors will usually be able to help eligible clients with an application: the relevant DSS form is **SF200**, and will be supplied either by the funeral director or the local Social Security office. The Social Fund payment will make provision for a standard funeral, including a hearse and one limousine, an inexpensive coffin, removal of the body to the funeral director's premises, use of the chapel of rest, all necessary preparations and arrangements and a funeral director and four bearers. It will also pay for travelling expenses *either* to register the death or to attend the funeral, but not both; a reasonably priced floral tribute will be paid for, and up to £75 for special religious requirements (such as taking the coffin into church the day before a funeral). For further information, read the helpful DSS booklet **D49** *What to Do After a Death* (or *What to Do After a Death in Scotland*).

A number of local authorities now provide a municipal funeral service. This is done by contracting with local funeral directors for the provision of simple, low-cost funerals for residents of the local authority area. The London boroughs of Lambeth and Lewisham operate such a scheme, and a similar one exists in Cardiff. The cost is considerably less than that of an average local funeral.

Relatives of a member of the armed forces who dies in service may receive help with funeral costs from the Ministry of Defence (see **Chapter 16**).

When someone without relatives dies, and no one can be found to pay for the funeral, the local district council where the person died (or hospital, if the death occurred in hospital) is responsible for arranging the funeral and paying for the cost. If the police have a body in their charge for which no relative can be traced, they notify the local authority who will then provide a minimum price funeral. Many hospitals have a 'funeral fund' and most local authorities have contracts with local funeral directors for the provision of such funerals. Arrangements vary considerably in different areas. If the provision of such a funeral is likely to be needed, acquaintances of the deceased must not approach any funeral director to begin making funeral arrangements. If they do, responsibility for funeral costs will then fall upon them, as local authorities have no power to reimburse costs where a third party has already made funeral arrangements. The local authority may recoup the cost of the funeral from the estate of the deceased, or from anyone who was responsible for maintaining the deceased while still alive.

Finally, most funeral directors are sympathetic to clients with little money who have to arrange a funeral, but do not meet the criteria for a grant from the Social Fund. Most funeral directors will provide a basic funeral at minimum cost; it is sometimes possible to spread this cost over a number of monthly payments. The funeral director should be told at the outset if there are financial difficulties, and ways will usually be found to give practical assistance.

CHAPTER 9

BURIAL

WHEN someone dies, arrangements for the funeral can be made very quickly, but the date and time should not be confirmed until the death has been registered, and the registrar's certificate for burial (or the coroner's order for burial, should the coroner be involved) has been issued. This must be given to the funeral director; without it, the funeral cannot proceed.

Burial in churchyards

Anyone, whether Christian or not, whose permanent address is within the ecclesiastical parish, is in theory entitled to be buried in the parish churchyard, even if he or she dies away from the parish. In practice, there may be no space left in the churchyard. Many old churchyards are closed for further burials, but some churches have burial grounds separated from the church, where parishioners have the right of burial. Ex-parishioners and non-parishioners with family graves or whose close relatives have been buried in the churchyard have the right of burial there, as does anyone who dies within the parish.

It is the incumbent (vicar, rector or priest in charge) and the parochial church council who decide whether to allow someone who has no right by law or custom to burial in the churchyard to be buried there, and what fee to charge. For a non-parishioner, or someone with no connection with the parish, the charges are likely to be higher than for a parishioner.

Burial fees

For people who live within the boundaries of the local parish, certain fees are payable to the local church for funeral services in church followed by burial in the churchyard. A proportion of these fees is paid to the incumbent, and the remainder to the parochial church council; these fees are specified by the Church of England under the Parochial Fees Order, and usually increase annually.

Currently (1994), the fee payable for a funeral service in church is £43, and the fee for subsequent burial in the churchyard is £70: a total of £113. If the church service is followed by burial in a municipal or private cemetery, the church fee of £43 remains the same, but the interment fee is paid to the local authority or owners of the cemetery and will vary considerably; no interment fee is payable to the church. Any payment for an organist, choir or bell ringers is additional; there is often a charge for heating and for the services of a verger. The fee for burial in a churchyard without having had a service in a church of the parish beforehand is £85; the same fee is payable if the churchyard burial does not immediately follow the church service, but takes place on a subsequent occasion. If a graveside service is held before the burial, the fee of £43 remains; the cost is the same as if the funeral service were to be held in the church. No fee is payable for the burial of a stillborn child, or for the funeral or burial of an infant who died within one year of birth.

If, after cremation, the ashes are to be buried in the churchyard, different fees apply. If the ashes are to be buried loose, that is, the turf removed and the loose ashes poured into a shallow plot ('strewing'), the fee is £57; if the ashes are to be buried in a casket or urn, the fee increases to £70. If the crematorium service has been a simple committal and the funeral service is to be held in the churchyard when the ashes are buried, a further fee of £43 is incurred. This fee does not apply, however, if the incumbent attends the burial of the ashes and provides a simple service of committal.

Gravediggers' fees are in addition to the above. If the parish has its own gravedigger, the fee will be between £60 and £100; if the funeral director provides the gravedigger, the fee is likely to be between £90 and £140. These fees vary according to place and circumstances, and are likely to rise annually – sometimes considerably.

The grave

Paying a burial fee does not buy the right to choose the location of the grave in the churchyard. The vicar allots the site. Nor does the burial fee entitle you to ownership of the grave or to the exclusive right of burial in that grave.

By faculty

If you want the exclusive use of a plot in a churchyard, you must apply to the diocesan registrar to reserve a grave space, by a licence called a faculty. Although a faculty gives the right to say who can be buried in the plot, the freehold of the ground continues to belong to the church.

The fee charged by the diocese for a faculty depends on the amount of work involved in the petition. It takes about six weeks for a faculty to be granted. When a person dies, it is too late to get a faculty for him or her, but the relatives could apply for a faculty to reserve the grave for other members of the family. Anyone arranging a burial in a grave reserved by a faculty must produce the faculty or other evidence which proves the right to the grave.

The incumbent charges a fee for the first and each subsequent interment in a grave reserved by faculty. An additional charge is made for removing and replacing an existing headstone to enable subsequent interments in a grave to take place.

Burial inside a church

Today, any rights an incumbent may have had in the past to consent to a burial inside the church building have become obsolete. Faculties to permit such burials are rarely granted and in urban areas burial in and under a church is prohibited by law.

Burial in cemeteries

Most cemeteries are non-denominational, and are run either by a local authority or by a privately owned company. A few cemeteries are owned by a particular denomination; burial in such places is usually restricted to members of that denomination.

Some cemeteries have a section of the ground consecrated by the Church of England, while the opening of many new cemeteries (the old ones are filling up) is attended by a service of consecration for the whole of the area.

The fee payable to an Anglican clergyman for performing a burial in a cemetery or crematorium is the same as that for a funeral service in church: £43. There is no church fee, however, if the burial immediately follows a church service. Should the cemetery burial take place some time after a funeral service in church, an interment fee of £12 is payable in addition to the £43 fee for the church funeral service.

Some cemeteries have ground dedicated to, or reserved for other specific religious groups, and a separate section of general ground. In most cemeteries, any type of religious service (or none at all) can be held. Most cemeteries have a chapel which is non-denominational, and can be used for funeral services when a service in the church is not desired. However, it should be noted that many of these are seldom used, and a considerable number have neither lighting nor heating, and may be damp and somewhat dilapidated.

Some cemeteries provide the services of a chaplain for burial services on a rota basis; where this is in effect, there is usually a choice of Roman Catholic, Church of England or Free Church.

Fees

Fees for burial in a cemetery vary widely even within the same locality. They are set by the owners, under the terms of the appropriate Acts of Parliament. Fees and regulations are usually displayed at the cemetery. If you write to the superintendents of the local cemeteries, you will be sent lists or brochures, from which you can compare the charges and conditions. A cemetery's fee may include the services of a clergyman and gravedigger; some will not allow flowers to be planted or put on graves; others will not permit any monument or memorial to be put up, except over the more expensive graves or for a limited number of years only, after which the cemetery authorities can remove it. Conditions or payments for maintenance are often stipulated.

In most local authority cemeteries, a higher fee is required for those who are not residents within the local council district; these are usually double the normal fees, but may be treble, or even more. There may be some concessions for former residents and their relatives. Interment fees are less for children than for adults; each cemetery authority fixes its own fees and defines its own age limits.

Cemetery burial fees are usually in two parts; there is a charge for purchasing the exclusive right of burial in a certain plot and an additional charge for interment. These charges vary enormously, especially in inner cities. The purchase of an exclusive right of burial used to be known as 'buying a plot'; most authorities will sell a lease on a plot for a certain period of time, so that only the purchaser or his or her family can be buried there. The terms of the lease were traditionally 99 years, but 75 years is now common, and some exclusive rights of burial are available for only 50, or even 25 years.

Most local authority cemeteries have an application form which the executor or next of kin is required to sign. All fees have to be paid in advance, and all the required documents sent to the cemetery office a stipulated time before the funeral. This will normally be dealt with by the funeral director; the client will then have the fees added to the funeral account, and repay the funeral director on presentation of the account after the funeral.

Graves

In most cemeteries, there are various categories of grave.

The cheapest are graves without the right to exclusive burial. The person paying the interment fee has no right to say who else may or may not be buried in the grave. The graves are marked by a number; it may be possible to put up a small memorial or plaque. In some cemeteries, no interments will take place in such a grave for a set number of years – usually seven or 14 – after the last burial, except to bury another member of the same family.

In a few cemeteries, for a small fee a grave space can be reserved for a specified number of years from the date of payment. After this, it reverts to the cemetery unless a further fee has been paid either to reserve the space for a further period or for the exclusive right to the grave on behalf of the person buried in it, so that it becomes similar to a private (or purchased) grave.

In most cemeteries, you can buy the right of exclusive burial in a particular plot, in a similar way as by a faculty granted for a grave in a churchyard. The right used to be in perpetuity, but nowadays it is more usually granted for a specific number of years – for instance, 50.

For a private grave, you get a deed of grant (sometimes referred to as a certificate of ownership), for which some cemeteries make a small charge. The deed should be kept somewhere safe and the family or executors should know where it is. It may have to be produced in evidence before the grave can be opened for an interment. Usually the signature of the owner of the grave is required on the cemetery's application form to authorise the opening of a private grave. If the owner of the exclusive right of burial has died, the cemetery will probably require some alternative formality to authorise the use of the grave if the right had not been re-registered following the death of the owner. Afterwards, the deed will be endorsed with details of the burial and returned to the executors. An interment fee has to be paid in addition, and also a fee for removing and replacing an existing headstone.

Another category of grave is the 'lawn grave', in which you have the right to exclusive burial, but can only put up a very simple headstone, leaving the rest of the grave as grass. Kerbs, surrounds, and elaborate memorials are not permitted. This type of grave enables easier maintenance, and consequently most modern cemeteries permit lawn graves only. Enquiries must be made as soon as possible if anything other than a simple headstone is envisaged, as considerable distress could be caused if an elaborate memorial is planned and restrictions are only discovered after the burial has taken place.

On cemetery plans, various categories of grave are shown; where this is applicable, fees will depend on the type, size and depth of the grave. In older cemeteries, normal unlined graves are referred to as 'earth graves'; 'brick graves' have a bricked (or concrete) floor and walls and are much more expensive. Where these are still available, longer notice of burial and higher interment fees are often required.

Formalities and the construction of a brick grave can take weeks; these are now very unusual.

DOCUMENTS FOR BURIAL

Registrar's certificate for burial (the disposal certificate) *or*	from registrar	required before burial can take place	via relative and funeral director to burial authorities; Part C returned to registrar
If inquest is to be held: Coroner's order for burial	from coroner	authorises burial	
Application for burial in cemetery	from cemetery via funeral director, usually signed by executor or next of kin	applies for burial and confirms arrangements	to cemetery authorities
Grave deeds *or* Faculty	from cemetery *or* diocese	proves right to grave	to burial authorities
Copy of entry in burial register	from burial authorities	proves burial and locates grave	to executor or next of kin

Burial at sea

Burial at sea is both complicated and expensive, but it is possible at certain places along the coast of the UK. For further details, see **Chapter 16**.

Other burial grounds

If you want to be buried in ground other than a churchyard or cemetery, the law stipulates that such private burials must be registered. Even if you are the freeholder of the land, you must ascertain from the deeds whether the land is restricted in the use to which it may be put. If you want to bury someone in your garden, you must apply for and obtain permission from your local planning authority, and the local environmental health department must be notified and given the opportunity to object to the proposal.

CHAPTER 10

CREMATION

IN MOST areas, the majority of funerals involve cremation rather than burial. This is due not only to the fact that cremation is cheaper, but also to a radical shift in attitudes which has developed since cremation began to be popular in the early years of this century. Before cremation can take place, the cause of death has to be ascertained beyond any reasonable doubt. If the deceased's doctor knows the cause of death, he or she will sign the medical certificate of the cause of death, and an additional certificate of examination which must be corroborated by another doctor. If he or she does not know the cause of death, the coroner must be informed and, ultimately, will issue a coroner's certificate for cremation. Unlike burial, which can sometimes take place on the authority of a disposal certificate issued before registration, cremation cannot take place until the correct certificates have been produced and the death registered.

The formalities

Four statutory forms have to be completed before cremation can take place; one by the next of kin or the executor, the others by three different doctors. The forms are issued by the crematorium; funeral directors keep a supply and doctors usually keep a supply of those relevant to them.

Form A is the application for cremation, and has to be completed by the next of kin or the executor, and countersigned by a householder who knows him or her personally. In most situations, the funeral director will be acceptable as counter signatory, but some crematoria insist on someone else signing the form.

Forms B and **C** are on the same piece of paper, which also often includes **Form F**. **Form B** has to be completed by the doctor who attended the deceased during the last illness; he or she must examine the body before the form can be completed. This may or may not be the patient's normal GP. The doctor may have to ask the relatives or acquaintances for some of the information the forms require; for instance, whether the deceased has undergone any operation during the final illness, or within a year before death, whether the deceased had a pacemaker, and whether or not it had been removed (pacemakers must be removed before cremation to avoid an explosion).

Form C is the confirmatory medical certificate, and must be completed by a doctor who has been registered as a medical practitioner in the UK for five years or more. He or she must not be a relative of the deceased, nor a relative or partner of the doctor who completed Form B. If two hospital doctors complete Forms B and C, they must not have worked on the same ward, attending the same patient. The second doctor also has to see the body before completing the form.

Form F, the fourth statutory document, has to be signed by the medical referee of the crematorium, stating that he or she is satisfied with the details on Forms B and C, or the coroner's certificate for cremation. The medical referee has the authority to prevent cremation taking place and may query details given in the forms supplied. If it is felt necessary, he or she may order a post mortem to take place, or refer the matter to the coroner, if this has not already been done. The relatives of the deceased have no right to prevent this post mortem; if they do not wish it to take place, then they must forego cremation and opt for burial instead. If they do agree to the post mortem, it is quite likely that they will have to pay for it. This is extremely unusual, however: the funeral director and crematoria staff will usually notice any anomalies before it reaches the stage of submission to the medical referee. Most crematoria include the fee for the services of the medical referee in the total charge for cremation.

When the coroner is involved and has ordered a post mortem, he or she will issue a certificate for cremation for which there is no charge; in this case, Forms B and C are not required. When a death is reported to the coroner, he or she must be informed at the outset if the funeral is to involve cremation, so that the appropriate certificate may be issued. This is statutory **Form E**, and (if there is to be no inquest) will be supplied as a pink form to the relatives so that they may register, and as a yellow form to the funeral director for submission to the crematorium. Sometimes the appropriate forms may be sent by the coroner direct to the registrar and crematorium.

In very rare cases where the coroner has a reason for not allowing cremation to take place, he or she will issue a coroner's order for burial only. The coroner may be able to inform the relatives that cremation may be possible at a later date, when the investigations have been completed; the relatives in this case must be prepared to wait for cremation at a later date, or opt for burial.

If the body of a stillborn child is to be cremated, a special medical certificate has to be completed by a doctor who was present at the birth, or who examined the body after birth. No second medical certificate is required, but the medical referee still has to complete Form F. Many crematoria charge no fees for the cremation of stillborn children, or for infants up to the age of one year.

Fees

Fees for a cremation funeral include the charges made by the crematorium, the fees for the doctor's certificates and, normally, a standard fee for the minister who takes the service, and the organist. All these are normally paid in advance by the funeral director, and added to the final funeral account.

The fees charged by crematoria vary from one district to another, but are generally in the region of £100 to £150, with additional fees charged for those who did not live in the local district. Unlike burial fees, these are not usually doubled, but involve only a small extra charge.

The doctors who prepare and sign Forms B and C are each entitled to a fee; the British Medical Association fixes a minimum fee on an annual basis. The fee for each part was £31 in 1994, and is likely to rise each year. A fee may also be charged by a doctor for removing a pacemaker before cremation, although this may be done by the funeral director's staff as part of the inclusive charge.

Sometimes, when death has occurred in hospital, the hospital wishes to carry out a post mortem to further its own understanding. The consent of the relatives must be obtained for this and, if given, Form C will not be required – providing the post mortem is carried out by a pathologist of not less than five years' standing and the result known by the doctor who completed Form B. Thus, only one fee of £31 will be charged, unless the pathologist was of less than five years' standing, in which case another doctor must complete Form C and the full £62 will be chargeable.

Most crematoria charge reduced fees for the funerals of children up to school-leaving age; practices vary, but the fees are often in the region of 20 per cent of the full adult fees. As already stated, there are usually no fees for stillbirths or infants up to about one year old.

Crematoria

The majority of crematoria are run by local authorities, although some are privately run. Each crematorium has its own scale of fees: considerable variation exists. Many have brochures giving details of what they offer, and the fees involved: most organise annual 'open days', usually on a Sunday, when the general public can investigate the whole cremation procedure. Most crematoria are open Monday to Friday only; a few are open on Saturday mornings, and some will be prepared to offer cremation outside normal working hours at an extra charge, which is usually quite considerable.

The service

Charges for cremation usually include a fee for the use of the crematorium chapel, whether or not it is used for a religious service. The chapel is non-denominational and will cater for other religions as well as Christian. Some crematoria have a rota of chaplains of various denominations, but usually arrangements for a clergyman to conduct the funeral service will be made by the relatives or the funeral director. There is no law requiring a religious service at a funeral, and a small but growing number of people opt for a non-religious funeral service. The British Humanist Association★ or the National Secular Society★ will be happy to put you in touch with someone in your area who can conduct such services; most funeral directors will be able to refer you to someone, and some are experienced themselves at conducting such services.

Most crematoria have facilities for playing music while the congregation enters and leaves, and this may be chosen by the relatives.

Crematoria work to a strict appointments system, so any service has to be fairly short, unless a special booking is made for a longer period, for which an extra charge will be made. Most crematoria allow 30 minutes between appointments, some allow 45 minutes, and some only 20 minutes.

Memorials

Most crematoria have various forms of memorial. There is usually a 'Book of Remembrance' in which the name of the deceased may be suitably inscribed; other memorials involve small stone wall-plaques, memorial rose-bushes with a plaque giving the name of the deceased, or a display of spring flowers. Few now provide a columbarium, where ashes may be stored in a small niche in a special wall.

All of these will involve special charges, and are usually offered to the bereaved a couple of weeks after the funeral.

Cremated remains

The cremated remains, or ashes of the deceased, may be scattered in the grounds of the crematorium, taken away to be scattered elsewhere, or buried in a local churchyard or cemetery. The crematorium will not normally charge a fee for scattering ashes shortly after the funeral, but a fee will be incurred if the ashes are stored and scattered at a later date. There will also be a fee – about £25 – if the ashes are to be scattered in the grounds of a different crematorium than the one where the funeral took place.

DOCUMENTS FOR CREMATION

Document	Source	Purpose	Destination
Registrar's certificate for burial or cremation (green certificate) or	from registrar	required before funeral can take place	via relative and funeral director to crematorium authorities; Part C returns to registrar
Coroner's certificate for cremation: Form E	from coroner after post mortem or inquest	replaces Form B/C	
Form A	from funeral director or crematorium to be completed by executor or next of kin	applies for cremation and confirms arrangements	to crematorium
Form B*	from doctor or hospital	certifies cause of death	to medical referee at crematorium
Form C*†	from doctor or hospital, to be completed by second doctor	confirms cause of death	to medical referee at crematorium
Ashes Disposal Form	from funeral director or crematorium	confirms arrangements, gives instructions for disposal of ashes	to crematorium authorities
Form F	from medical referee	confirms information in Forms B & C or E	to crematorium authorities
Certificate for disposal of cremated remains	from crematorium	confirms date and place of cremation	via relatives to burial authorities
Certificate of cremation for burial or scattering	from crematorium	copy of entry in register	to executor or next of kin

*Forms B and C are not required if the coroner is involved and issues Form E
†Form C is not required if a hospital post mortem is conducted by a doctor qualified for more than five years

The Church of England charge for burial of loose ashes is £57, and for burial of ashes contained in a casket or urn £70 (1994).

Most crematoria are not able to arrange for the transport of ashes to another locality. The funeral director will be able to arrange this or a local courier or parcels services will do it within the UK for a fee of around £10 upwards.

A leaflet, *Questions People Ask*, answering queries about cremation, is produced by the Federation of British Cremation Authorities, and is available from some crematoria.

CHAPTER 11

BEFORE THE FUNERAL

MOST funeral directors maintain a 24-hour service; if a death occurs at home or in a nursing home out of office hours, two members of the funeral director's staff who are on duty at that time will come very quickly to take the body to the mortuary. Nursing and retirement homes normally want the body moved as soon as possible. It is rare, these days, for a body to remain at home for the interval between death and the funeral, although it is possible if the relatives request it. Unless the relatives intend arranging the funeral themselves, the funeral director should be approached as soon as possible after the death occurs. In many cases, the member of staff with whom you have the first interview will remain in charge until after the funeral is completed.

The body

About 80 per cent of people currently die in hospital, and half of the remainder in nursing or retirement homes. Of the remaining 10 per cent who die at home, the great majority are taken to the funeral director's premises to await the funeral in a chapel of rest; this is a small room where the deceased remains in a coffin until shortly before the funeral. Normally, laying out, or 'first offices' (known as 'last offices' in hospital) almost always takes place at the funeral director's mortuary. Unless requested to dress the body in its own clothes, the funeral director will supply a funeral gown as part of the inclusive service. He or she will want to know what the family would like to do as far as jewellery is concerned.

When someone dies in hospital, the body is taken to the hospital mortuary. It remains there until cremation papers (if needed) are completed, or until any post mortem has been attended to. The hospital will not require the body to be moved from the mortuary out of normal working hours; if the coroner is involved, it cannot be moved until he or she is satisfied that the necessary papers can be issued.

When the funeral director's staff come to remove a body from a house or hospital, they normally use a large estate car adapted for the purpose. Sometimes an ambulance is used; very rarely, a hearse. The staff will normally use a covered stretcher; sometimes, a form of coffin designed for removals called a 'shell'. The funeral director usually needs written authority in order to remove a body from hospital; this normally takes the form of the green certificate issued by the registrar (Registrar's certificate for burial or cremation), which means that registration must be attended to as soon as possible. An authorisation signed by the next of kin or executor is sometimes acceptable.

When the body is kept in a chapel of rest, relatives and friends can go to see the body before the funeral; the funeral director will usually ask for an appointment to be made so that a member of staff can be available to give the family undivided attention. Sometimes extra charges are made for viewing the body in evenings or at weekends. Relatives often like to leave some personal memento in the coffin, but are embarrassed to ask; funeral directors will often suggest that photographs, letters, flowers etc. may be placed in the coffin with the deceased. Where cremation is involved, it is important that these mementoes are combustible.

Some larger firms of funeral directors also have their own chapel for private prayer, in which a religious service can be held at the beginning of the funeral, before the cortege leaves for the cemetery or crematorium.

Embalming

Embalming is a process intended to delay temporarily the process of decomposition, and involves replacing the blood in the arterial system with a preservative, normally a solution of formalin. The process is similar to a blood transfusion, and is sometimes called 'preservative' or 'hygienic' treatment. It bears no resemblance to the ancient Egyptian process of mummification.

Embalming is advisable if the body is to be returned to a private house to await the funeral, or if the funeral is to be held more than four or five days from the date of death, and the body cannot be kept in cold storage. Some bodies begin to decompose much sooner than others; a bad appearance and odours can be extremely distressing for a family who wish to view the body. Some funeral directors embalm every body brought on to their premises, while others do so only if they consider it necessary. Sometimes there is an extra charge for embalming. If relatives of the deceased do not want the body to be embalmed, they should discuss the matter with the funeral director.

Before a body can be embalmed the doctor must have completed the medical certificate of the cause of death; where cremation is involved, Forms B and C must also have been completed. If the coroner is involved, embalming must not take place until his or her authority has been obtained. An embalmer should be qualified by examination, and abide by the code of practice laid down by the British Institute of Embalmers. In the UK, embalmers tend to make minimal use of cosmetics (unless requested to do so by the family); the aim is to present as natural an appearance as possible, as if the deceased were asleep.

In a hospital mortuary, the bodies are kept refrigerated; most funeral directors also have cold-storage facilities, sometimes combined with deep-freeze facilities so that bodies can, if necessary, be kept for some considerable time before the funeral takes place. This may be necessary where a member of the family is abroad and cannot be contacted, or where a close relative is in hospital awaiting recovery.

Final arrangements

The funeral director must have the registrar's disposal certificate (or the coroner's equivalent authorisation) before confirming the final arrangements. He or she will see to it that all official forms are completed and taken to the right people at the right time. For a burial, for instance, he or she takes charge of any grave deeds and gets a cemetery's form of application signed by the executor.

In effect, the funeral director should co-ordinate the various operations at the different stages. He or she will approach the person in charge of wherever it has been decided the burial or cremation is to take place (this usually means the local clergyman or superintendent of the cemetery or crematorium) in order to reserve a time and, for a burial, to order the type of grave you want.

For a cremation, the funeral director sees that a relative or the executor completes the form of application and the form giving instructions for disposal of the ashes and will also arrange for two doctors to complete Forms B and C. He or she will pay them their fees and, when the necessary forms have been gathered, will get them to the medical referee at the crematorium.

Most crematoria produce at least one other form on which the person organising the funeral confirms any details already provisionally arranged, such as the date and time of cremation. Some crematoria ask for specific instructions about the disposal of the ashes on this form; others have yet another form for this.

The forms have to be submitted to the medical referee of the crematorium by a stipulated time – which is never less than 24 hours before the cremation is due. The reservation of a time for the cremation is accepted subject to the forms reaching the crematorium within the specified time limit and the fees being paid in advance.

The fees – to vicar, sexton, gravedigger, organist, choirmaster, chaplain and officials at the cemetery or crematorium, as the case may be – usually have to be paid in advance. The funeral director will make the actual payments and will add the charges to the total account.

Service

Either the funeral director or a member of the family should ask whoever the family wants to officiate at any service, whether he or she is willing to do so and whether he or she will be available at the time planned for holding the ceremony. The minister will probably visit the family, particularly if the deceased had an active church connection, to offer consolation and also to arrange practical details of the service.

There is no obligation to have a service in church, and a service can be held in the churchyard or cemetery. An Anglican burial can be taken by the incumbent or, with his or her permission, by any other clergyman, such as a friend of the family or the clergyman whose church the deceased normally attended.

If you want a particular piece of music to be played, you should ask for this when making arrangements for the service.

A service in a crematorium or cemetery chapel is restricted by the time allowed – normally half an hour.

Most religious denominations have some form of funeral ceremony. In England, unless the dead person had professed another religion, one of the Church of England services will probably be said at his funeral.

Rituals can be adapted according to the preferences of those concerned. For instance, the main part of the service can be said in the church or at the funeral director's with only a few words of committal at the graveside, or all the service can be at the grave. A funeral address may be given either in the church or outside, or not at all.

If you are having an unusual form of service, you can arrange through the funeral director or officiant for special service sheets to be printed.

Other denominations

Denominational burial grounds usually insist on their own form of service. If you are arranging the funeral of someone of a faith different from your own, get in touch as soon as possible with the equivalent of the local parish priest of that denomination to find out what needs to be done. (See also **Chapter 13**).

With Orthodox Jews, the body should be buried as soon as possible once the disposal certificate is issued. If a man subscribes to a synagogue burial society, he or his wife or his dependent children will be buried, free, by the society in its cemetery. The funeral and coffin will be very simple, and there will be no flowers. Orthodox Jews do not get cremated, and embalming or bequeathing a body for medical purposes is not allowed. Reform non-orthodox Jews are more flexible, and permit cremation. The funeral will always be simple, but flowers are allowed. A Jewish burial society may agree to carry out the funeral of a Jew who was not a member of a synagogue and had not been subscribing to any burial society, but his family will be charged for the funeral and the cost will be considerable. There is rarely any difference between the funeral of members of the same synagogue; all are simple. If a Jew dies when away from home, it is the responsibility of the relatives to bring the body back at their own expense for the synagogue burial society to take over.

For a practising Roman Catholic, it is usual to arrange for the priest to say a requiem mass in the local parish church and for him to take the funeral service. There are no set fees laid down for Roman Catholic priests to charge for funeral services, but it is usual for the deceased's family to make an offering to the church. Cremation is no longer discouraged for Roman Catholics, and crematoria have Roman Catholic priests on their roster.

Non-religious service

There is no necessity to have a religious ceremony, or indeed any kind of ceremony at all, at a funeral. However, because some kind of religious ceremony is customary, if you do not want one or the dead person had made it clear that he or she did not want one, it is important that the executor or whoever is in charge of the arrangements makes this known well before the funeral.

If a body is to be buried in a churchyard without a religious ceremony, or with a ceremony held by an officiant of another denomination, you should give the incumbent of the parish 48 hours' notice in writing; in practice, it should be possible to make the necessary arrangements in a telephone conversation. The usual parish regulations and fees still apply.

If a body is to be buried in a cemetery or cremated at a crematorium without a religious ceremony, tell the funeral director or the authorities at the time the funeral is being arranged. There will normally be no difficulties, provided it is clear that the proceedings will be properly conducted. Where there is not going to be a religious ceremony, whoever is in charge of the funeral arrangements must also make arrangements for the details of the ceremony.

If you want no ceremony at all, the usual procedure is for a few members of the family or close friends to attend the committal in silence or with some music being played. If you want a non-religious ceremony without an officiant, on the lines of a Friends' meeting, you must make sure that those present either know already how such a ceremony works or are told at the beginning.

The more usual procedure is to have an officiant who prepares and conducts the ceremony, on the lines of a minister. This may be a member of the family or a close friend, or a representative of an appropriate organisation or a sympathetic religious minister. The only qualification is some experience of handling meetings. Business, professional and labour organisations generally contain such people, as do humanist societies.

The national freethought organisations in London all give help with funerals: they can offer information and advice by telephone or post, send out literature, and sometimes provide officiants for funerals. The British Humanist Association* has a network of humanist funeral officiators who can be contacted by calling the 24-hour national helpline. Other agencies include the National Secular Society*, the Rationalist Press Association* and the South Place Ethical Society*. The British Humanist Association charges £3 for its booklet *Funerals Without God, a Practical Guide to Non-religious Funerals*, and the other organisations appreciate donations for their material. Officiants would expect to be paid a standard fee plus expenses, normally about the same as the fee set for church ministers.

A non-religious ceremony may take any form, provided it is decent and orderly. The usual procedure is for the officiant to explain the ceremony, after which there may be readings of appropriate prose or poetry, tributes either by the officiant or others present, and the playing of appropriate music. It is common to allow a time of silence where the deceased may be remembered personally, and religious people may offer silent prayers. These ceremonies are not intended to oppose religious funerals, but are alternatives for people who would feel it hypocritical to have a religious service, or who want a respectful celebration of the death that has occurred without a religious emphasis.

Press notices

Announcements of deaths are usually made in local papers, and sometimes the national dailies; the cost for an average obituary in a local paper is likely to be about £20, and in a national paper about £100 to £150. Newspapers will not normally accept text for obituaries by telephone, unless placed by a funeral director; even then there is a rigorous call–back and checking system because of many distressing hoaxes. The papers do not usually ask for evidence that the death has occurred, unless the notice is submitted by someone who is not a relative, executor, or funeral director.

National daily newspapers will insist on a standard form of announcement, and will restrict the words that can be used. Most funeral directors are well aware of the system, and will advise accordingly. The address of the deceased should *not* be inserted into the obituary: too many houses have been burgled while the funeral is taking place. Where there is anxiety about this, the funeral director may be able to supply a member of staff as a 'house sitter' for the duration of the funeral service.

The majority of funerals currently give people the opportunity of making donations to a nominated charity in memory of the deceased, as well as or in place of flowers. It is normal for the funeral director to collect such donations and forward them in due course to the charity concerned, informing the relatives of the amount collected. This information is usually contained in the obituary, and the funeral director's name and address is given so that information can be given and donations made.

Details of the date, time and place of the funeral can be included in the obituary. Anyone who has not been specifically invited but wishes to attend is expected to arrive independently at the time and place announced in the press. If the family want to restrict attendance at the funeral, the obituary should state 'private funeral service', or the equivalent; in this case, only those invited by the family should attend. If the family think that a great many people may wish to attend, arrangements may be made for a funeral service in a large church or auditorium followed by cremation or burial which is attended only by the family and close friends; alternatively, a private funeral for the family only may be followed some time later by a memorial service and all who wish to pay their last respects to the deceased may attend. If no details of the time or place are published, it should be assumed that the funeral is to be private.

Flowers

The press notice should make clear whether there are to be no flowers, family flowers only, or the option of a memorial donation. A 'no flowers' request should be strictly observed. Flowers are normally sent to the funeral director's premises; most florists are aware of this, and will contact the funeral director to ask what time flowers should be delivered. It is not normal for press notices these days to say where flowers should be sent: the funeral director will collect any that are sent to the family home when he or she calls at the house for the funeral service, and will normally supply the family with a list of those who sent flowers when submitting the account. Flower cards may be collected and returned if the funeral director is asked to do so.

When a body is buried, flowers are normally left on the grave after it has been filled in. At the crematorium, there will normally be restrictions as to where flowers can be placed, and the length of time they will be displayed: some are on display for only 24 hours after the funeral, others for a week, and others are regularly cleared once a week. Traditional wreaths are rare these days; it is common for the family to request flowers in the form of bouquets or arrangements that can be taken to hospitals or old people's homes after the funeral service has been completed.

CHAPTER 12

THE FUNERAL

TRADITIONALLY, the cortege (or funeral procession) started at the house where the deceased lived, with the hearse and one or more cars for the mourners travelling by a pre-arranged route to the church or crematorium. This still frequently happens, but it is as common for the hearse to travel directly to the location of the funeral from the funeral director's premises; the mourners will then be brought to meet it either by their own or the funeral director's vehicles. If the funeral director provides cars for the bereaved relatives, he or she will marshal the cortege and arrange when it shall start.

Timing is very important, because cemetery and cremation authorities work to a very tight schedule; if the funeral cortege arrives too early or too late, it will probably interfere with the preceding or following funerals. Should it arrive considerably late, especially at the crematorium, it is possible that the funeral service will have to be drastically shortened, or even postponed, to the great distress of the relatives.

The funeral director should discuss all the details of the funeral with you beforehand, and arrange where people are to be taken after the funeral, whether the minister requires transport, what happens to the flowers etc.

If you are worried that the house may be burgled while the funeral is taking place, the funeral director may be able to provide a member of staff as a 'house-sitter'. The funeral director should not incur any additional expenses without the client's authority.

It is unlikely these days that the funeral director will ask relatives if they would like to witness the closing of the coffin immediately before the funeral, but customs vary in different parts of the country.

The funeral director may walk in front of the hearse at it leaves the deceased's house, and again as it approaches the church or crematorium; this is not only as a mark of respect, but to enable him or her to direct the traffic and keep the funeral cortege together, especially as it leaves a side street to enter a main road. The coffin will normally be carried into the church or crematorium on the shoulders of four of the funeral director's staff, although in some places a small trolley is used for moving the coffin. Sometimes, members or friends of the family are able to act as bearers; this enables a more personal participation in the funeral, and the funeral director's staff will still be on hand to assist and give directions. Occasionally, at more formal funerals, pallbearers walk alongside the coffin, apparently fulfilling no purpose. Traditionally, these used to carry the 'pall', a heavy fabric canopy which was held over the coffin. Today, the pall is normally used to cover the coffin in the hearse if it has to travel some considerable distance between towns before the funeral cortege can gather; it is then removed, and the family flowers are placed on the coffin before moving off.

Burial

Where a burial is preceded by a church service, the coffin is taken in to the church by the bearers and placed on trestles or a trolley in front of the altar. In Roman Catholic and some other churches, the coffin may be taken into church before the funeral, often the previous evening, and remain there until the funeral service takes place. Most funeral services in church take about half an hour, although a requiem mass, or the funeral of a well-known member of the church congregation, may take an hour or more. After the service, the bearers will take the coffin from the church, either to the churchyard or, more commonly, to the local cemetery, usually led by the minister and funeral director. If burial is not preceded by a church service, the coffin is carried direct from the hearse to the graveside, where there is normally a short service.

The coffin will be lowered into the grave by the bearers while the words of committal are said; this part of the funeral service is quite brief, and normally lasts about five minutes. In Scotland, the coffin is usually lowered by members of the family. Sometimes the mourners throw a token handful of earth into the grave, or each drops a flower on to the coffin; they do not normally (except in Ireland) remain to see the grave filled in – this is done later by the cemetery staff or gravedigger.

A register of burials in the parish is kept by the church; every cemetery has to keep a register of burials and records of who owns a grave plot, and who has already been buried in each grave. Copies of entries can be obtained for a small fee.

When someone is buried in a churchyard the family is responsible for looking after the grave. The PCC (parochial church council) is responsible for looking after the churchyard generally, and for keeping the paths and unused parts tidy. Some dioceses stipulate that, before a funeral takes place, a contribution must be made towards the upkeep of the churchyard. Municipal and private cemeteries will employ groundsmen to take care of grounds and graves; this upkeep is often difficult and costly, which is why most authorities now stipulate lawn graves only: graves with a simple headstone in line with other headstones, and no kerbs or surrounds to interfere with mechanical mowing. However, where there are gravestones, whether simple or elaborate, the holder of the grave deeds is responsible for their upkeep; this can become very expensive as stones weather and crack, and ground settles over the years. Upkeep of memorial stones is often neglected – another reason why authorities prefer to stipulate lawn graves only.

Many churches place quite rigid restrictions on the type of memorials and stone which may be used in churchyards. It is essential to check with the local church before placing an order with a stonemason; funeral directors will be aware of the requirements of local churches and will be able to advise accordingly.

Cremation

Traditionally, the funeral service prior to cremation was held in church, with the congregation (or only the chief mourners if the cremation was to be private) travelling to the appropriate crematorium for a brief committal afterwards. Increasingly, funeral services are held entirely in crematorium chapels; the hearse and cars go straight to the crematorium and the bearers carry the coffin into the chapel and place it on the catafalque. Usually, the mourners follow the coffin into the crematorium, led by the minister and funeral director but, increasingly, people prefer to enter the chapel and sit down before the coffin is brought in.

When the words of committal are spoken, the coffin passes out of sight; it will either sink into a recess, pass through a door or a curtain will move in front of it. Some people prefer the coffin to remain on the catafalque until the mourners have left the chapel; this option is available if requested. During the funeral service, the funeral director's staff will take flowers from the hearse and place them in the floral display area; when the coffin moves out of sight at committal, the flowers on the coffin will be retrieved and added to the display. Some crematoria will only keep flowers on display for the day following the funeral; others leave them in place for several days, while yet others clear them once a week. The funeral director will take appropriate sprays and arrangements to hospitals or nursing homes after the mourners have departed if requested to do so: these are often greatly appreciated.

When the coffin moves out of sight, it is taken to the committal room to await cremation. Each coffin is loaded individually into a cremator, once the name on the coffin plate has been checked by the crematorium staff. It is illegal to remove the coffin from the crematorium, or (other than the flowers) anything from the coffin, once the committal has been made. When the cremation process is complete, after two to three hours, the ashes are refined separately and placed in carefully labelled containers; each cremator must be cleared totally before another coffin can be loaded.

When making arrangements for the cremation, the next of kin or executors can ask to be present when the coffin is placed in the cremator; this is especially relevant for Hindu funerals, where traditionally the next of kin would light the funeral pyre. Usually, two people only are allowed.

Each crematorium has to keep a register of cremations. A certified copy of the entry in the register is obtainable for a small fee. It is unlikely that such a certificate would be necessary, unless the death had not been registered in this country, or the ashes were being sent to another country which required such a certificate.

The ashes

When making arrangements for the funeral, the clients will be asked what they would like done with the ashes. Most are scattered, or buried loose beneath the turf in the crematorium grounds; they can, however, be taken away by the next of kin or executor for disposal elsewhere: for example, scattering in a place meaningful to the deceased or family, or burial in a churchyard or cemetery. If a family grave already exists, the ashes may be buried in that grave for a fee, usually around £50. If a plot for the burial of ashes has to be purchased (i.e. where no family grave exists), there will (except in churchyards) be a fee for the exclusive right of burial. Cremated remains can usually be obtained from the crematorium on the day following the funeral; however, providing notice is given in advance, ashes may be obtained on the same day if the funeral takes place before midday.

Crematoria are not normally willing to post or otherwise send cremated remains to other locations. However, most funeral directors will take them short distances by car or arrange for national transportation by a courier. It is difficult and expensive to send them by post yourself but if you wish to do so you should consult one of the national parcel services. Costs are usually between £10 and £20 inland, and about double to Ireland or any of the UK coastal islands.

Most crematoria will arrange to store ashes until they are required for a monthly fee; funeral directors will do the same, but most will probably not charge for storage. Funeral directors will also supply caskets for burial of ashes, or simple urns for storage or scattering. These vary in price from about £10 for a simple urn to over £100 for an elaborate casket. Decisions about or arrangements for the eventual disposal of ashes need not be made at the time of the funeral. However, if there is even the remotest likelihood that the crematorium will *not* be required to scatter the ashes in their grounds, this should be made clear at the outset. It is easy to scatter ashes later, but, obviously, impossible to do anything else with them once they have been scattered. Normally, at the time of signing statutory **Form A**, the next of kin or executor will be required to fill in a form on the reverse giving instructions for the ashes.

When the ashes are taken away, the crematorium normally provides a free certificate confirming that the cremation has taken place. This document has no legal significance, but is sometimes requested by church or cemetery authorities when the ashes are to be buried.

If ashes are to be scattered in the grounds of a different crematorium, or the same crematorium at a considerably later date, there will be an additional fee of around £10–£30. If a funeral director has to arrange for ashes to be buried in a different location or at a considerably later time, he or she will charge a fee in addition to the inclusive fee for the funeral.

There is no law regulating the disposal of cremated remains; ashes can be scattered anywhere, providing the scattering is done respectfully, and with the consent of the owners or executors of private grounds, such as golf courses etc. The funeral director will arrange to scatter the ashes for clients in a chosen location and will not normally charge for this unless considerable time and travelling expenses are incurred.

The crematorium grounds are usually known as a 'Garden of Remembrance'; such ground is not usually consecrated, and the place is not normally marked. Some crematoria scatter the ashes around on the surface of the grass or earth; others remove a small portion of turf, pour the ashes on to the ground and then replace the turf. The family can sometimes choose a spot and witness the proceedings if they request to do so; some crematoria charge a fee for this. There is generally no formal ceremony.

The Church of England will frequently only allow ashes to be buried in churchyards; they may be buried loose (as described for crematoria) or in a casket; fees for this were £57 and £70 respectively at the time of writing (February 1994). Most churches will allow the placement of a small plaque, inscribed with the name of the deceased, where the ashes are buried; as with headstones, there are usually rigid restrictions about the type and size of stone that is accepted. Each church tends to have its own interpretation of regulations, and it is essential that enquiries are made at the appropriate church. A fee will be charged for placing the memorial stone, either in churchyard or cemetery.

A final word: if scattering the ashes yourself, it is important to ensure that the mourners stand with the wind behind them.

CHAPTER 13

FUNERALS FOR DIFFERING FAITHS

THE multi-ethnic society in which we live means that, especially in many inner city areas, a large number of funerals will not conform to the traditional Christian approach, but will vary considerably according to the religion of the group concerned. It is not possible within the scope of this book to adequately cover all aspects of the different faiths now represented in the UK, and what follows is a considerably simplified outline.

Moslems

Moslems live according to a strict moral code which has specific prescriptions concerning death and burial. There are numerous Moslem sects, each with its own variation of funeral rites, but in the UK about 90 per cent are Sunni Moslems, and the remaining 10 per cent are almost entirely Shia Moslems.

Moslem communities will normally appoint one person to represent them in making funeral arrangements, who will usually deal with one approved funeral director in the locality. The representative will advise of strict rules, which need to be followed as closely as possible.

Moslems are always buried, never cremated. Traditionally there is no coffin – the body is wrapped in a plain white sheet and buried within 24 hours of death in an unmarked grave, which must be raised between 4 and 12 inches from the ground, and must not be walked, sat or stood upon. British law requires a coffin for burial or cremation, which has now become acceptable.

Many British cemeteries insist on levelling the graves as soon as possible, which has led to some authorities providing special areas for Moslem burials; where this is not so, great distress can be caused for the families concerned. Because of the need for haste in burials, requests for post mortems and organ donation are usually, but not always, refused.

Moslems believe that the soul remains for some time in the body after death, and the body remains conscious of pain. Bodies must therefore be handled with great care and sensitivity, and disposable gloves worn at all times by those handling the body: the body must never be touched directly by a non-Moslem. Embalming is not normally practised, but is permissible where the body has to be conveyed over long distances.

Normally, the family will attend to laying out the body, and they will turn the head over the right shoulder to face Mecca, which is roughly to the south-east. The body will be wrapped in a plain sheet and taken home or to the Mosque for ritual washing: men will wash male bodies, and women female. Camphor is normally placed in the armpits and body orifices, and the body will be clothed in clean white cotton clothes or a special white shroud brought back personally from Mecca.

The funeral service will take considerable time. There will be ritual washing, at least 30 minutes of prayer at the Mosque, possible return to the family home, prayers at the graveside and the filling in of the grave. Relatives and friends will carry the coffin at shoulder height, passing it from one to another, and they will want to see the face of the deceased after the final prayer at the graveside. Moslems must be buried facing Mecca, with the head over the right shoulder; hence graves must lie north-east/south-west, with the head at the south-west end. The family will normally perform all rites and ceremonies, together with the imam, the spiritual leader of the local mosque.

Hindus

Unlike Moslems, there is not normally any insistence on one approved funeral director to handle funerals; there is no central authority for those who adhere to this religion, and rites and customs vary enormously.

There are thousands of Hindu deities, which are all held to be manifestations of the same God. The three main deities are Brahma, the Creator; Vishnu, the Preserver; and Shiva, the Destroyer. Hindu belief in reincarnation means that most individuals face death in the hope of achieving a better form in the next round of life. Death is therefore relatively insignificant, although there is likely to be open mourning with much weeping and physical contact by family and friends. There are normally strong objections to post mortem examinations, which are held to be deeply disrespectful to the dead.

Hindus are always cremated, and never buried. Prior to the cremation, most Hindus bring their dead into a chapel of rest, where the body must be wrapped in a plain sheet and placed on the floor. Most light lamps or candles, and those who come to view will probably burn incense sticks. There are normally no objections to the body being handled by non-Hindus, but this and all burial rites are capable of great variation. The family concerned will be explicit about the rites required by its form of Hinduism.

Sikhs

Sikhism developed from Hinduism in the fifteenth century, and has much in common with it, but with a strong emphasis on militarism. There is a common belief in reincarnation, and the fact of death is normally accepted calmly.

There are five symbols of faith which are vitally important to every Sikh. The *Kesh* is the uncut hair which, for men, is always turbaned. The *Kangha* is a ritual comb to keep the hair in place; this is never removed. The *Kara* is a steel bracelet worn on the right wrist (or left if left-handed); the *Kirpan* is a small symbolic dagger, which may actually vary in size from a brooch to a broadsword – and the Sikh will never be separated from it. Finally, the *Kaccha* are ceremonial undergarments which are never completely removed, even while bathing. Sikhs are always cremated, never buried; the Sikh family will insist in every instance that their dead are cremated with all five 'K symbols' present. Considerable diplomacy may be required to satisfy both family and crematorium authorities.

After death, men are dressed in a white cotton shroud and turban; young women are dressed in red, and older women in white. The family will almost always want to lay out the body, and will want cremation to take place as soon as possible – in India, it would normally be within 24 hours. The coffin will usually be taken home and opened for friends and family to pay their last respects and will then be taken either to the *gurdwara* for the main funeral service, or direct to the crematorium, where the oldest son will, instead of lighting the traditional funeral pyre, press the crematorium button or see the coffin into the cremator. The ashes will be required for scattering in a river or at sea; it is not unusual for one member of the family to take them to India to scatter them in the Punjab.

Stillborn babies, by exception, are usually buried.

Buddhists

Buddhism is the main religion in many far-eastern countries such as Burma and Nepal, but it is still relatively rare in the UK. After death, Buddhists will have the deceased person wrapped in a plain sheet and prepared for cremation. Buddhists of different nationalities have widely varying funeral customs, and nothing can be assumed to be held in common.

Jews

Scattered from their homeland by the Roman Army in AD70, the Jews dispersed across the world and adopted many different practices and interpretations of the Mosaic Law, yet always maintaining their essential unity. Orthodox Jews believe that the Law was literally handed to Moses by God, while Progressive Jews (divided into Reform, Liberal, and Conservative groups) believe that the Law, while inspired, was written down and influenced by many different authors. Orthodox Jews are thus extremely strict on the observation of funeral rites, while Progressive Jews vary in their attitudes.

When a Jew dies, the body is traditionally left for eight minutes while a feather is placed on the mouth and nostrils to give any indications or signs of breathing. Eyes and mouth are then closed by the oldest son, or nearest relative. Many Jews follow the custom of appointing 'wachers', people who stay with the body night and day until the funeral, praying and reciting psalms. The dead are buried as soon as possible. No Orthodox Jew will accept cremation, although it is becoming increasingly favourable among some Progressive groups. Orthodox rabbis will sometimes permit the burial of cremated remains in a full-sized coffin, and say *Kaddish* (the mourner's prayer) for the person concerned.

Jewish funerals are either arranged by a Jewish funeral agency (such as United Synagogues), or a contract will be arranged with a Gentile funeral service, under the terms of which all local Jewish funerals will be arranged according to strict rabbinical control. If a secular Jew is appointed as executor, or is responsible for making funeral arrangements, it is essential that enquiries are made into the religious background of the deceased, so that the appropriate rabbi may be contacted. Jewish coffins are as simple and plain as possible, usually with rope handles and written nameplates. Embalming does not take place, and mourners do not view the body.

Christian cults

There are now a great variety of Christian cults, or diverging Christian groups, which include the Mormons, Jehovah's Witnesses, Christadelphians, Christian Scientists, Scientologists, the Moonies and the Children of God. For most, while differences in doctrine are held to be immensely important, there is little deviation from orthodox Christian practice as far as funerals are concerned. Funerals may well take longer, which may cause difficulties in fitting in with crematorium schedules.

Some groups, such as Bahai and Hare Krishna, are basically Hindu derivants, and may adhere more to Hindu funeral rites than any other.

Much New Age culture is basically a westernised form of Hinduism, and those who practise yoga or transcendental meditation may adopt the Hindu philosophies which lie behind them, which will in due course affect the funeral arrangements that will need to be made.

CHAPTER 14

Arranging a funeral without a funeral director

When a close relative dies, most people prefer someone else to undertake the responsibility of arranging the funeral and attend to all the necessary details. Most want to 'get the funeral over with' as soon as possible, and are reluctant to be involved any more than is necessary in making arrangements for, and participation in the funeral service. However, human reactions to grief follow a fairly standard pattern (see **Chapter 18**), and it is an established fact that personal involvement in arrangements for the funeral assists the grieving process and hastens a healthy recovery.

Such participation will, for most people, seldom involve more than laying out and dressing the deceased, viewing the body in the chapel of rest, providing family bearers to carry the coffin and participating in the funeral service. It is, however, perfectly possible to arrange the whole funeral yourself; there can be considerable snags and difficulties, but with knowledge and determination, these can be overcome.

Arranging the funeral

Assuming that the coroner is not involved, the doctor's medical certificate of the cause of death must be obtained, and the death registered. The necessary papers must be obtained, completed and submitted to the cemetery or crematorium with the appropriate fees. A date and time for the funeral must be arranged with the same authorities – if a church service is to be held, the church and minister must be consulted before that time is confirmed. If a minister is to conduct the funeral service, he or she must be approached and asked to do so, again before confirming the time. A coffin must be obtained, and a decision made about where the body is to be kept until the time of the funeral. Means of conveying the coffin to the church, cemetery or crematorium must be obtained. If the funeral is to involve burial, a gravedigger must be hired, or the decision taken to dig the grave oneself. If the grave is to be on private land (i.e. not in a churchyard or cemetery), the local planning authorities must be informed and permission sought. Bearers must be found to carry the coffin.

These constitute the necessary minimum; several of the above involve statutory forms and legal documents, all of which can be dealt with but which require patience.

Cremation

Cremation is a much more common option than burial – currently, 80 per cent of funerals involve cremation.

You must first obtain two doctor's certificates for cremation to take place (**Forms B** and **C**, both on the same piece of paper). If the deceased died in hospital, the hospital must be asked for the papers; if death occurred at home, the doctor who had been attending the deceased must complete Form B and another, independent, doctor complete Form C. Each doctor will require the standard fee for signing (£31 in 1994).

The next of kin or executor will need to obtain statutory **Form A** from the crematorium; this is the application for cremation, and will be accompanied by the crematorium's own administration form. Both must be completed and submitted to the crematorium with the doctor's forms B and C, the registrar's green certificate for burial or cremation, and the appropriate fee. Many crematoria also require a signed form giving instructions about the disposal of cremated remains; this is often printed on the reverse of Form A, but is not a statutory form and is not itself part of Form A.

The crematorium's administration form will include a signed declaration that the coffin to be used will conform to legislation relating to pollution of the environment (a coffin *must* be used: cremation without a coffin will not be permitted). This is important: people have in the past constructed their own coffins, brought them to the crematorium at the designated time, only to be refused permission to cremate because the coffins did not conform to the necessary requirements. These requirements are usually printed on the crematorium's application form, but in any case can be obtained from the local crematorium.

Burial

Burial has fewer problems than cremation, provided it is to take place in a churchyard or cemetery. No doctor's certificates (Forms B and C) are required, but the registrar's green certificate for burial or cremation must be submitted to the church or cemetery authorities, together with, in the case of a municipal or private cemetery, a completed application form and the required fee. A date and time for the funeral must be agreed. A grave-digger must be found and hired: the churchyard may have its own gravedigger.

Coffin

For those with some knowledge of d-i-y, a suitable coffin can be made at home. It must be strong enough to cope with the stress imparted by an inert body being shouldered and lowered by inexpert bearers, and (in the case of cremation) be made of suitable materials. Many d-i-y enthusiasts have seen home-made chairs collapse and shelves fall off walls: it is far from funny when a coffin collapses at a funeral. If the necessary experience and expertise are there, then go ahead, but *no one* should contemplate beginning a d-i-y career by making a coffin.

Waiting for the funeral

A decision must be made as to where the coffined body is to be stored until the funeral takes place. This will usually be one room of the house, which will need to be kept as cool as possible. Ensure that all heating is turned off, and that there is constant ventilation. Some diseases cause bodily decomposition to begin far quicker than normal: it may be necessary to arrange for the body to be embalmed, especially in summer. Portable air-conditioners may be hired from an equipment-hire company to help keep the temperature low.

If the deceased died in hospital, it may be possible to arrange for the body to remain in the hospital mortuary until the day before the funeral.

Funeral transport

The coffin can be taken to the funeral in the back of a large estate car, land rover or horse and carriage. Hearses and horse-drawn hearses can be hired if preferred. It is unwise for bearers to carry the coffin any further than is strictly necessary.

Burial at home

It is possible to arrange for a burial to take place on your own land – in a garden or field. Permission from planning authorities must be obtained, and may be refused if the proposed burial site relates adversely to the water table. Local authorities may well be extremely reluctant to agree to the burial; such proposals involve grey areas of the law, and almost always cause considerable discussion and argument. If such a private burial is to be considered, it should be discussed with the appropriate authorities long before death is expected to take place.

Should permission be granted, there are still considerable difficulties to be faced. For example, if relatives of the deceased decide for any reason to move house, the presence of a grave in the garden presents problems. The emotional decision to leave the grave must be faced, as must the fact that its presence will mean that the selling price of the house will almost certainly drop by between 25 and 50 per cent. If you want to take the body to a new location, a Home Office licence for exhumation will be required; this will be expensive, involve a long wait after application and require that the work be done at a specific time by a Home Office-approved contractor. Exhumation without such a licence is a criminal offence.

Unless a small part of private grounds can be set aside in perpetuity as a private cemetery, which may well be possible on an estate or farm, arrangements for burial at home are likely to be fraught with difficulties. There will be legal and practical problems, and most planning authorities have good reasons for being very unhappy about the idea. A reasonable solution to this problem is to arrange for a cremation, and then to scatter or bury the ashes in the garden or field. Technically, an ashes casket buried in private ground is subject to the same laws of exhumation as a coffin; it can, however, legally be moved from one part of the private grounds to another.

Funeral management schemes

Many funeral directors are eager to see their clients more involved in funeral arrangements, being aware that this will assist them in the grieving process. Some offer a service to clients who want to arrange funerals for their relatives themselves, and are prepared to sell them a coffin at a reasonable price, hire out a hearse if so required and provide a management service for a set fee. The service would provide all the necessary documentation, with advice on how and where to make the necessary arrangements.

If, however, a client decides to pay a management fee, buy a coffin, hire a hearse, and then decides to pay the funeral director or hospital mortuary staff to prepare the body, rent a chapel of rest etc., the overall cost will probably be more than if a funeral director had been asked to make all the necessary arrangements in the first place.

Helpful advice on organising a funeral yourself can be obtained from The Natural Death Centre★. The centre also publishes the *Natural Death Handbook*, which gives advice and information on all aspects of arranging and conducting funerals yourself. This can be obtained from the Centre at a cost of £10.95 including postage and packing.

CHAPTER 15

AFTER THE FUNERAL

WHEN the funeral service has finished, family and friends often gather for light refreshments at the house of the deceased, at the house of another member of the family, or at a local public house or restaurant. If required to do so, the funeral director will arrange for caterers to come into the house during the funeral and provide for guests. Mourners need to be clearly informed about what has been arranged, and where they are to go.

Paying for the funeral

The funeral director will submit an account fairly soon after the funeral, and will appreciate payment as soon as possible – he or she has already paid out quite substantial sums to various bodies to enable the funeral to take place – but will, of course, understand if the account cannot be settled until a grant of probate or letters of administration have been issued (you must make this clear). All the major banks will release funds from frozen accounts to enable the funeral bill to be paid, if provided with a suitable funeral account from the funeral director. Legally, payment of the funeral bill is the first claim on the estate of the deceased, taking priority over income tax and any other claims.

The funeral director's account should be as detailed as possible, showing separately what has been paid out to doctors, crematoria, ministers etc. on your behalf, and what is due to his or her company as the fee for professional services rendered. This will enable you to verify that only authorised payments have been made. Any gratuities given to mortuary or cemetery staff by the funeral director are normally considered as part of the inclusive charge; any tips to bearers or others officiating at the funeral would be at the discretion of the client.

All the payments that the funeral director will have made on behalf of the client should be expenses that would inevitably have been incurred; in addition to the necessities, he or she may have been asked to provide flowers, place obituary notices in newspapers, provide catering and service sheets etc.

The services of the funeral director, minister and cemetery or crematorium are exempt from VAT. VAT must, however, be paid on flowers, catering, printing, and any form of memorial.

Memorials

Relatives often want to place a memorial tablet or headstone in a churchyard or cemetery where a coffin or ashes casket has been buried. Both churchyards and municipal cemeteries impose restrictions on the size and type of memorial and on the kind of stone that may be used and the type of lettering inscribed on it. Many cemeteries and almost all churchyards currently prohibit kerbs or surrounds to graves, and memorials are often restricted to a headstone or a plinth and vase set at the head of the grave.

Neither reserving a grave in a churchyard by faculty (where this is still possible) or purchasing the exclusive right of burial in a cemetery provides the right to putting up any kind of memorial. For this, approval must be gained from the respective authority and a fee paid. The Church Commissioners in the Parochial Fees Order lay down the charges for memorials in the churchyards of the Church of England. Fees in 1994 were as follows:

- small wooden cross   £8
- vase (not exceeding 12″ × 8″ x 8″)   £19
- tablet for cremated remains (up to 21″ x 21″)   £33
- any other memorial, including inscription   £77
- additional inscription, added later   £18.

Anything other than a simple headstone or inscription requires the granting of a faculty. The wording of an inscription must be approved by the incumbent; most will object to colloquialism and informal descriptions, and generally stipulate that any quotations are biblical or otherwise religious.

The funeral director is frequently involved in these arrangements, and will warn clients of any restrictions he or she knows about. Some funeral directors provide their own service of monumental masonry; almost all have contact with stonemasons whom they use as subcontractors.

Arranging for a memorial

The funeral director or monumental mason will normally apply to the church or cemetery authorities for permission to erect a memorial; a copy of the entry in the burial register or the deeds of the grave may be required before authority is given.

After a burial, several months should be allowed for settlement before any memorial is erected or replaced. Time should be taken in the consideration and purchase of a memorial; unsolicited memorial salesmen should be ignored. Names of established local firms of monumental masons can be obtained from the National Association of Memorial Masons★ or the Memorial Advisory Bureau★.

Do not, under any circumstances, order a memorial from any source before ascertaining exactly what the burial grounds' regulations are.

The cost of memorials varies enormously, depending on the type of stone, size, ornamentation, finish and lettering. Before ordering a memorial, ask for a written estimate which states clearly the items and total cost, including any delivery or erection charges and cemetery fees. It is normal for the stonemason to ask for a 50 per cent deposit to be paid by the client on confirmation of the order: this may seem a lot, but if the client changes his or her mind, there is not much the mason can do with the already-inscribed stone.

VAT is charged on the provision of a new headstone or on adding a new inscription to an old one; it is not levied on the removal and replacement of existing memorials. The cemetery fee for the erection of a memorial is also exempt from VAT.

After cremation

About a week after a cremation has taken place, the crematorium will usually send a brochure to the next of kin explaining what kind of memorials are possible. These are all optional, are not covered by the fees paid for cremation, and are subject to the payment of VAT.

The most popular means of memorial at the crematorium is the 'Book of Remembrance'. Hand-lettered inscriptions in the book usually consist of the name, date of death, and a short epitaph; the charge depends on the length of the entry. The crematorium displays the book, open at the right page, on the anniversary of death, or of the funeral. Some crematoria sell a miniature reproduction of the entry in the form of a card, or bound as a booklet, the price of which depends on the quality of the presentation.

Charges for the erection of memorial plaques or for inscriptions on panels in memorial passages, where available, vary greatly. Some municipal crematoria will allow no memorial other than the entry in the Book of Remembrance.

Some crematoria have a colonnade of niches for ashes called a columbarium; the ashes are either walled in by a plaque or left in an urn in the niche. Most of these are now full, and where there are spaces, charges are high.

Other crematoria have memorial trees, or rosebushes; these are usually arranged in beds, where the memorial bush is chosen by the family, the ashes scattered around it, and a small plaque placed nearby. Costs vary, as does the length of time for which the crematorium will provide maintenance before another charge is made.

Charitable donations

An increasing amount of people ask family and friends to make donations to a nominated charity in memory of the deceased, and regard this as a fitting memorial for the person concerned. Usually, the funeral director will collect and forward donations to the appropriate charity, sending receipts to each donor and providing the charity and family with a list of donations received. The funeral director will not normally charge for this service.

CHAPTER 16

AWAY FROM HOME

AS PEOPLE move from place to place more often nowadays, they often express a wish to be buried or cremated in a district other than the one in which they died. In such cases, funeral arrangements have to be made in two places: where the death occurred, and where the funeral is to take place. Most funeral directors are accustomed to this, but if the distance involved is too great, the funeral director may subcontract arrangements at the other end to a colleague on the spot.

Bodies are normally conveyed by hearse within the UK, as this is the quickest and cheapest form of transport. It is quite possible to send a coffin by rail or air, but it is likely to be much more expensive: the coffin must be packed in a strong wooden crate and covered with hessian – this adds to the size and weight, and therefore to the cost. Charges vary according to the distance and route covered, but airlines may charge double or treble the normal cargo rates, or may charge a special rate for carrying a coffin with a body inside.

The crated coffin must be accompanied by all the necessary documents for the funeral and the body must be embalmed if it is to be conveyed by any form of public transport. It is also normal practice to ensure that a body is embalmed before carrying it any considerable distance by hearse. Most funeral directors will deal with a distant funeral by accompanying the hearse and driver, and hiring bearers at the other end from a local colleague.

Registration must be effected in the registration district where the person died, and not where the funeral is to take place.

Death abroad

When a British subject dies abroad, whether as a resident or as a visitor, the death must be registered where he or she died according to local regulations and customs. In many countries, the British Consul can also register the death: this has the advantage that certified copies of the entry in the Register of Deaths can eventually be obtained from the General Register Office*, just as if the death had been registered in the UK. This will not happen automatically; the appropriate consul must be approached and asked, and it will be some time before a death certificate is available in the UK. There is otherwise no official record of the death in this country, although before the funeral can take place, the registrar of the relevant district must be asked to issue a certificate of no liability to register. For this, a copy of the foreign death certificate, suitably translated into English, must be supplied, giving the cause of death. The funeral director will normally be able to attend to this.

Death at sea

When a death occurs on a foreign ship, it counts as a death abroad; the death must be recorded in the ship's log, and the port superintendent where the ship's crew are discharged must make enquiries into the cause of death.

When death occurs on a British-registered ship, the death is recorded in the captain's log, and all facts and particulars relating to the death must be recorded and delivered to the Registrar General of Shipping and Seamen*, when arriving at any port within or outside the UK.

When a body is brought into a British port, the death must be reported to the coroner in whose jurisdiction the port is located. He or she may decide to order an enquiry, in which case the body cannot be moved without his or her consent. The registrar of the district in which the funeral is to take place must also issue a certificate of no liability to register, for which either a copy of the entry in the captain's log or a death certificate must be obtained. Copies of log entries can be obtained from the shipping company which owns the ship concerned, or the port superintendent where the body was brought ashore. Copies of the death certificate may be obtained from the Registrar General of Shipping and Seamen★. This will normally all be dealt with by the funeral director.

Death in the air

When death occurs in an aircraft, the death must be registered in the country to which that aircraft belongs. At the next landing following the death, the captain must notify the local police authorities, and the appropriate registration authority, which may not be in the same country as the one where the aircraft has landed. Subsequent action concerning arrangements for the body vary according to local regulations, but as far as relatives are concerned, the procedure to be followed is the same as that for a death which occurs abroad. These arrangements can be extremely complicated, and will normally be dealt with by the funeral director in conjunction with a specialist repatriation service.

Returning a body from abroad

When someone dies abroad and the body is to be returned to this country, the process is complex and expensive. Holiday or travel insurance which covers repatriation is essential, as the cost can run to several thousand pounds. If death occurs, there is usually an emergency telephone number on which to contact the insurance company or travel agency; the tour operator or British Consul in the area will be able to advise, although they will not be able to assist financially. If there appears to be no one to advise, it would be wise to telephone a reputable funeral director in the UK to ask for advice and assistance; most funeral directors are experienced in these matters, and can turn to specialist repatriation services if they need help.

The death must be registered in the country and area concerned, and death certificates and the doctor's medical certificate of the cause of death obtained. The local judicial authorities may want to investigate and, in any case, authority must be obtained from them to move the body out of their country. The body must be embalmed before it can be moved, and a certificate of embalming will be required. The body must be contained in a metal-lined coffin, which in turn must be covered with hessian and contained in a strong wooden crate. All necessary papers for customs clearance must be obtained, and arrangements made with an airline to convey the body to the UK.

Insurance companies will have contracts with repatriation services or firms of international funeral directors who will attend to all of this; if there is no insurance, it is possible for relatives to attend to the matter, but specialist knowledge and a great deal of patience is required, and the matter would be better entrusted to a UK funeral director. On arrival in the UK, customs clearance must be obtained; this may take several hours, but, once cleared, the body must be removed from the airport as soon as possible.

If death has occurred due to natural causes, the coroner will have only minimal involvement. If death is not due to natural causes, but is the result of an accident, the coroner in whose jurisdiction the airport lies will want to hold an inquest, and the body may not be moved from the mortuary until permission is given.

The registrar of the district in which the funeral is to take place will need to be informed, so that a certificate of no liability to register may be issued. For this, evidence of death and the cause of death will be required.

Funerals involving burial

If the funeral is to involve burial, all the documents received with the coffin must be taken to the registrar in the district where the funeral will take place, with the relevant papers suitably translated. The funeral director will normally attend to this, or the coroner's office may be able to help. The registrar will issue a certificate of no liability, which takes the place of the green certificate, and is the only document required by burial authorities, whether a church or local authority.

Funerals involving cremation

If the funeral is to involve cremation, the local registrar must issue a certificate of no liability as in the case of burial, but considerable further paperwork is involved. Application must be made to the Home Office* for authority to cremate; a certificate will be issued which will take the place of statutory **Forms B** and **C**. To obtain this, statutory **Form A** must be completed and signed, and taken to the Home Office with all documents received with the coffin: the foreign death certificate, embalming certificate, medical certificate of the cause of death, coroner's authority to remove the body from the country and, possibly, a 'freedom from infection' certificate. These may be sent or taken to Home Office, D Division.

Obviously, this will be time-consuming, and plans for the funeral must be adjusted accordingly. If sent by post, the envelope containing the papers should be marked 'Cremation papers: urgent'; it will be quicker to call in person. Normally, the funeral director will attend to this.

All documents received from or returned by the Home Office should then be taken to the local registrar in order to obtain a certificate of no liability; all these papers must then be submitted to the crematorium, although certain papers, such as copies of foreign death certificates, will probably be returned.

When the coroner is involved

If death appears to have been caused by something other than natural causes, the coroner of the district where the airport lies must be informed. He or she may order a post mortem and, if satisfied that death did occur from natural causes, will then issue the necessary documents: if the funeral involves burial, the coroner will issue a certificate of no liability to register, which is all that is required; if cremation, he or she will issue the coroner's certificate for cremation, and the Home Office will not be involved at all.

If the coroner finds that death did not occur from natural causes, he or she will order an inquest to be held, the results of which may well be inconclusive due to the embalming or deterioration of the body and the inability to call witnesses. In this case, the funeral cannot be held until authority to do so is obtained from the coroner.

Sending a body abroad

When someone who has died in England or Wales is going to be buried or cremated in another country (including Scotland, Northern Ireland and the Channel Isles), permission must first be obtained from the local coroner. **Form 104** gives notice to a coroner of intention to remove a body from England, which will be supplied by the registrar or funeral director: normally, the funeral director will deal with this.

If the registrar knows before registration that the body is to be taken out of England, he or she will not issue a certificate for burial or cremation; if, however, such a certificate has already been issued, it must be sent to the coroner together with the 'out of England' form. Four clear days must normally elapse before the coroner gives permission on **Form 103**. However, in cases of urgency, a personal visit to the coroner's office with all necessary documentation and information concerning the death will, provided the coroner is satisfied, enable the form to be signed and the body removed immediately. If the coroner is already in the process of investigating the death, he or she will not release the body for removal from England until satisfied that it will not be required for further examination.

There are no legal restrictions on taking cremated remains out of the UK, but other countries may impose their own restrictions. For example, Italy is the most difficult: the ashes are treated exactly the same as a body, with all the same documents required, together with permission to import from the local prefect of police in the area of intended disposal. A hermetically sealed container is required, the sealing of which must have been witnessed by a representative of the consul. Greece treats ashes in the same way as an exhumed body, which may not be imported into the country until one year after death. France requires consular sealing of a hermetically sealed container bearing an engraved plate which gives the name of the deceased, date of death and death certificate number. India requires a High Commission permit.

For all other countries, enquiries should be made at the relevant embassy or consulate.

Making the arrangements

Making the arrangements to take a body into another country for burial or cremation is an extremely complex matter and should not be contemplated without expert help. Generally, the body must be embalmed (there are few exceptions) and contained in a metal-lined coffin which is covered in hessian and strongly crated. All necessary freight documents must be completed, and a death certificate provided for UK customs clearance. Consular requirements of the destination country must be met, and all documents required must be translated and authenticated at the relevant consulate: there will be a fee for this.

Consular regulations

Consular regulations vary, but usually only in certain respects; they also change frequently, so in every case enquiries should be made at the local consulate of the country concerned.

The requirements usually include:

- consular permission to take the body into the relevant country
- a copy of the certificate of death supplied by the registrar, suitably translated
- an official certificate stating the cause of death and a declaration that sanitary regulations for transporting the body will be met
- a certificate of embalming
- a declaration from the funeral director stating that the coffin contains only the body of the deceased and accompanying clothing and packing
- details of the route, flight number, and date of departure
- a 'freedom from infection' certificate (FFI)
- a certificate of exhumation and a copy of the Home Office licence to exhume, in the case of exhumed bodies
- a passport wherever it is necessary for the body to pass through another country on the way to its destination – this does not apply to air transport
- an insistence that a consul representative attends the sealing of the coffin or crate.

In addition, the consulate will also provide information about formalities that will be required on arrival of the body, and what arrangements must be made beforehand.

Burial at sea

Burial at sea may be requested by anyone; it is relatively unusual, fairly complicated and very expensive. All materials disposed of at sea require a licence under the Dumping at Sea Act 1974; this includes bodies, but in order to minimise stress to the bereaved, the government will, in place of issuing a licence, accept written notification from a funeral director that he or she intends to bury a body at sea.

The letter must contain the name and address of the applicant (normally the funeral director), the date and time period for which permission is required, and the information that a human body is to be disposed of at sea. This letter should be sent without delay to The Fisheries Inspectorate*.

Time must be allowed for a reply, and other documentation must be gathered. Registration must take place in the district where death occurred, and the application must be made to the coroner to remove a body from England on **Form 104**. A copy of the death certificate will be required, and a declaration as to whether death was caused by an infectious disease. The coroner's permission to remove the body, on **Form 103**, will also be required.

Permission from the District Inspectorate of Fisheries must be obtained, and will only be given for a very small number of specified locations, almost always outside the three-mile limit.

The coffin must be made from solid wood, have many holes drilled in it, and contain suitable heavy weights to ensure it will sink. Where such burials are preceded by a church service, the coffin should be covered with a pall.

Arrangements for a suitable vessel must be made, allowing for the fact that not only must a heavy coffin be carried and lowered into the sea in a respectful way, but also that a number of passengers will want to accompany it on the boat. Local harbour masters can be a source of relevant information; generally, however, all arrangements will be made by an experienced funeral director.

No documents are required for scattering or burying ashes at sea.

Death when in the armed forces

If a member of the forces dies serving abroad, the Ministry of Defence normally allows the next of kin the following choice:

- a funeral overseas with two people from the UK (normally the next of kin) attending, all at public expense
- repatriation of the body where practicable at public expense to a funeral director in the UK chosen by the family. Once the body has reached the funeral director, the family becomes responsible for the funeral. The Ministry of Defence provides the coffin and a grant of £295 to assist with the funeral expenses.

If a serviceman or woman dies in this country, the next of kin can choose to have:

- **a funeral at public expense**   This will be arranged and paid for by the Ministry of Defence, provided it takes place near to where the death occurred. (Exceptionally, because military funerals cannot be arranged in Northern Ireland, a member of the forces dying there can be buried anywhere in the UK at public expense)

- **a private funeral with limited military assistance**   The Ministry of Defence pays for the coffin and the conveyance of the body some distance from the place of death to a funeral director chosen by the family. Once the body has reached the funeral director, the family is responsible for the funeral. The Ministry of Defence pays a grant of £295 to assist with the funeral costs

- **a private-expense funeral**   The next of kin claim the body and make all the arrangements privately (including the provision of a coffin). In this case, the Ministry of Defence allows a grant of £475.

A member of the forces who dies while serving may be buried in a military cemetery by consultation with the appropriate cemetery authorities. This will only be arranged at public expense if there is a military cemetery near to where the death occurred.

If someone who was receiving a war disablement pension dies as a result of that disablement or was drawing a constant attendance allowance, the Department of Social Security may pay for a simple funeral. The next of kin should contact the local war pensioners' welfare office straightaway, before any formal arrangements are made.

CHAPTER 17

SCOTLAND

THE CERTIFICATE of registration of death which the registrar has given to the informant must be given to the person in charge of the place of interment or cremation. No part of the certificate is returned to the registrar.

Burial

In Scotland a grave is referred to as a lair. As in England, it is possible to purchase the exclusive right of burial in a cemetery or kirkyard plot, either in perpetuity or for a limited period. Kirkyards are administered by the local district (or islands) council. In Scotland cemetery chapels are rare.

At burials in urban cemeteries, silk-tasselled cords, called courtesy cords, are attached to the coffin. Specific mourners are sent a card beforehand inviting them to hold a cord while the coffin bearers take the strain of the lowering. In most country areas the cords actually take the weight. Courtesy cords are not used for the burial of cremated remains.

A pad or mattress is often put on top of the coffin as a development of the old custom of putting grass or straw over the coffin to muffle the sound of earth falling on the lid when the grave is filled in.

In Scotland by tradition women did not go to the interment in the graveyard after the church service. This practice has been abandoned by and large, although it still survives occasionally, especially in the older generation.

Cremation

The regulations and procedure for cremation are the same as in England and Wales since the Cremation Regulations 1965 brought these into line with those of Scotland.

Sending a body abroad

There are no formalities connected with the removal of bodies out of Scotland for either cremation or burial in another country, but you should ensure that the death has been registered in Scotland before moving the body out of the country. The procurator fiscal does not have to be informed.

If the body is being taken to England or Wales for burial, the certificate of registration (**Form 14**) or the standard death certificate must be produced for the registrar there.

No formal notice has to be given or permission sought when cremated remains are being taken out of the country.

Bringing a body from abroad

There is no need to produce evidence for the registrar in Scotland that the death took place elsewhere. If the body is coming from England or Wales, the person in charge of the place of interment or cremation in Scotland will require the coroner's form permitting the body to be removed.

When a body is brought into Scotland to be cremated there, the authority of the Secretary of State for Scotland must be obtained before cremation can be carried out. This means applying to the Scottish Home and Health Department*, with any supporting papers, such as a foreign death certificate.

Cremated remains brought into Scotland must be accompanied by a certificate of cremation issued by the crematorium.

CHAPTER 18

THE GRIEF PROCESS

DEATH alters the course of daily life for all those closest to the person who had died. If someone close to you has died, you must accept that things will change, whether the change is small or immense. Something irreversible has happened and your life must now follow a different course. You will face various experiences which will affect you in certain ways until, having worked through them, you arrive at a point where your life is once again moving steadily in a positive direction.

Normal grief

Bereavement is a very complex issue; this short chapter describes many of the phases that you may encounter when recently bereaved – any description of reactions to grief has to be simplified because of the enormous variation from person to person in coping with the situation. Nevertheless, the considerable amount of study which has taken place over the last 25 years has revealed much that is common to the great majority of people.

There is nothing unusual about grieving: it is 'normal' and most people will make a 'normal' recovery without a great deal of assistance. Some, however, get stuck somewhere in the process of recovery and need help; others (fortunately, only a few) are so affected by their bereavement that the grief process gets out of hand. In such cases, treatment as well as assistance is needed, counsel as well as care. The normal grief processes only are covered in this section to help you understand how you may be feeling.

Most of the time, bereavement causes a great deal of pain; many people do not acknowledge this, fearing that they will be marked out as weak and abnormal. Family and friends will often avoid people who have lost partners, parents, children or close friends, usually because they are embarrassed and do not know what to say. They excuse their feelings of embarrassment and helplessness by saying things like: 'Grief is a very private affair. I don't want to intrude.' So the bereaved are often deserted just when they need most support, which leads them to believe that it is their pain and tears that cause others to shun them; they therefore make determined efforts to 'be strong' and suppress their natural emotional responses. More than anything else, this hinders recovery from grief.

Reactions to grief

When loss has occurred and the bereaved person has been diverted from the accustomed course of life, a number of psychological forces come into effect. The different stages of grief that a person may go through include shock, sorrow, anger, apathy and depression, before the process of recovery can begin. Not everyone experiences all of these emotions, and some stages may last longer than others. In other words, everyone is different.

Shock: the primary experience
The initial effect of bereavement is shock. There is a numbness in which the rest of the world often seems to recede, leaving the bereaved person in mental limbo; a common feeling is of the world carrying on but the person no longer feeling part of it. This leads almost immediately into a stage of denial – the strong feeling that death cannot possibly have occurred, that the bereaved person is dreaming, that the doctors have made a mistake. This begins at the moment of loss and has its major impact during the first two to three days. At this stage, people can be very susceptible; this should be recognised and care taken when an important decision has to be made – especially regarding the arrangements for the funeral. Dates and times often have to be decided upon quickly, but sufficient time should be allowed before the funeral to avoid making the wrong decisions in haste.

When death occurs after a long illness, or where there was ill-feeling between the deceased and the bereaved, the initial response is a feeling of relief: the tension is at last over and done with. This may be accompanied almost at once by a sense of guilt for feeling relieved – talking about this to a sensible and trustworthy friend will help.

Sorrow: the underlying experience

Shock often overlaps with or is followed by feelings of sorrow – the sadness which develops as the person becomes aware that an irreversible loss has occurred. Sorrow and pining can have the effects of physical pain, often made worse by the belief that one is supposed to 'be strong' and not show any undue signs of emotional disturbance. At this point, the bereaved person needs to be free to express grief with the support of others who will not be embarrassed or try to suppress the person's tears. In order to make a good recovery, the bereaved person needs to feel this pain, express it and work through it in ways which are appropriate to his or her personality.

But initial sorrow is often accompanied by unreasonable guilt. People often feel guilty because they think they could have done more than they did – had they done more, perhaps the deceased person would not have died – and much reassurance and patience is called for. This often leads to people 'bargaining' with God or with life in general (for example, by promising to be good if only they can wake up to find that it was all a bad dream). The only way to help someone going through these emotions is to root the person firmly in reality, to talk about the death and to have the person visit the body in a chapel of rest, thus allowing a gradual acceptance of the situation to come about in a way that can be coped with.

The acute stage of this phase does not usually last for very long, and is sometimes over in two or three weeks. The sorrow will persist, but will generally subside into a numbing ache. The guilt (real or imagined) may well last for a long time.

Anger: the developing experience

Many people get very angry when bereaved, usually in an irrational manner. There is anger with God (for letting death happen), with friends and family (for not understanding or for not being bereaved themselves), with themselves (for not coping) and with the deceased (for having died and left them). Sometimes the anger comes before the sorrow and guilt, sometimes after, and is often compounded by a strong and irrational resentment and a certain amount of aggression (depending on the person's personality – a very mild person is unlikely to become extremely aggressive). Friends need a great deal of patience: they should let the person cool down, then listen to the anger without being defensive or argumentative.

This stage of the grief process can last from a few days to several months. It may continue to simmer in the background for a long time, resulting in outbursts of irrational anger at unexpected times. Those on the receiving end should remember that the anger is not directed at them and try not to feel injured or aggrieved.

Apathy, depression and recovery
When the anger calms down, a state of apathy often develops. The bereaved person displays indifference to what is going on round about and may show a considerable reluctance to make decisions. Patience and encouragement are needed continuously.

Or there may be feelings of depression. Most people can work through these normal feelings of depression with the support of friends and family; however, this support should not be allowed to turn into an unhealthy dependence on the help of others – it is important to encourage people by doing things *with* them rather than *for* them, so that they will once again be able to do things for themselves. Occasionally, depression can degenerate into acute depression, where professional assistance is called for.

Gradually, even when the pain of bereavement has been acute, a sense of acceptance grows and the bereaved person once again begins to take an interest in life. When it becomes possible for the person to make positive plans for the future and again find pleasure in everyday experiences, the bereaved person is well on the way to recovery. Life will never be the same again, but it can now be lived in a normal, healthy manner.

Other common reactions

Shock can also have physical effects, leading to quite genuine symptoms. These are often not recognised as being part of the normal grief process and, as a result, many recently bereaved people worry that they have a physical illness on top of the burden of bereavement.

Headaches are common, as are a continuously dry mouth, weakness, breathlessness, oversensitivity to noise, tightness in the chest and throat, a hollow feeling in the stomach, giddiness and nausea. Hair loss may also occur. Some people lose weight, others put it on; some people are constantly tired, even when they have had sufficient sleep and food.

There are often real feelings of fear, sometimes based on the person's anxiety that he or she will not be able to cope. Absent-mindedness and lack of ability to concentrate on anything for very long are also common: sometimes people forget what they were saying in mid-sentence. Memory is frequently affected: facts, names, experiences, all well known, cannot be brought to mind when needed, which can be very upsetting.

All of these are quite normal experiences, and recognising them as such will greatly assist you to live through them and come to terms with the reality of the bereavement which has occurred.

On the way to recovery

In practice, of course, it is seldom as simple as this. Some people do not appear to go through any of the emotional phases listed above, while others pass from feeling to feeling, only to repeat the process a few weeks later. Realising that there is no one certain way that you're *supposed* to feel will help you on your way to recovery.

CHAPTER 19

CHILD AND COT DEATHS

EVERY year, about 8,000 babies in this country die within the first month of life, or are stillborn; one couple out of every 500 has suffered this form of bereavement. Yet only recently has this experience been recognised as real bereavement; previously, parents who had lost new-born babies were expected to recover quickly from their loss.

Recent research has indicated, however, that mourning lasts longer among bereaved parents than in widows or widowers; in a recent survey of parents who had lost babies in the first few months of life, two-thirds of those interviewed felt that their main need was to have their baby recognised as a real person, and not as 'something that could be replaced'.

Memorials

Mourning involves memories, and when a small baby dies, memories are few. Until very recently, it used to be felt that the less the parents knew about the dead baby, the less they would grieve; the mother was often sedated, and the dead child whisked away before she or the father could see it. Relatives were advised to dispose of any potential reminders: baby clothes were removed, pram and cot disposed of and toys given away or carefully hidden. This deprived the parents of almost all the grounds of memory, thus making it almost impossible for them to find a degree of healing through mourning.

Active contact with the dead baby greatly helps to make it a real person to bereaved parents, and supplies at least some of the memories they need. Mothers are more often encouraged to hold their dead baby, and to wash and dress it. Photographs can provide memories and confirm the reality of a child's existence, thus providing a source of comfort. Expensive equipment is unnecessary: a simple photograph will do. A lock of hair can be kept, or a little down snipped from the baby's head and kept in a transparent envelope. Handprints or footprints can be taken with washable ink pads, and suitably mounted. A toy or two intended for the baby can be placed with it in the coffin.

The funeral

Parents who have lost babies or small children should be encouraged to resist the temptation to get the funeral over with as soon as possible. The funeral service is one of the few things which bereaved parents can arrange for their babies, and as much time and thought as possible should go into discussing the details. The Foundation for the Study of Infant Deaths* publishes a leaflet, *Information for parents following the unexpected death of their baby*, which contains lots of helpful advice. The funeral will cause pain, but this pain is a necessary part of the healing and recovery process.

Many, probably most, funeral directors will make no charge for arranging the funeral of a baby or small child; funeral arrangements, services of staff, use of the chapel of rest, an appropriate coffin and a hearse or estate car will normally be provided free. If elaborate funeral arrangements are requested, such as a solid wood coffin or cars for mourners, these will have to be paid for. Many hospitals now make provision for the reverent disposal of miscarriages or stillbirths, with a simple funeral service often taking place in the hospital chapel.

Most crematoria do not charge for the cremation of children under the age of one year: it should be noted that there will not normally be any cremated remains available for disposal afterwards, as the cremation process is usually total, leaving no ashes for disposal.

Many cemeteries also make no charge for the burial of infants under one year, and fees for burial in churchyards are frequently waived. Headstones or other memorial stones will, however, be subject to the same fees as adults.

Care agencies

A number of care agencies exist for the sole purpose of offering help and support to those who have lost babies and small children (*see the address section*).

CHAPTER 20

WHAT ELSE HAS TO BE DONE?

NONE of the property of the deceased should be sold, nor, strictly speaking, given away until probate has been granted. Probate is the official validation and approval of a will, and application must be made to the nearest probate court for approval before the intentions of the deceased can be put into practice. This will take at least several weeks. If the deceased left no will, 'letters of administration' must be applied for; this will take longer. For further details of how to administer an estate, see the Consumers' Association book *Wills and Probate*.

Until probate or letters of administration are granted, the deceased's executor must inform the bank, which will stop payment of all cheques and banker's orders; however, the major banks will generally release funds to pay the funeral account if presented with a legitimate account from a funeral director. The post office, building society, or any other institution where the deceased had an account must also be notified; any savings will be temporarily frozen. The tax inspector must also be informed that the death has occurred.

After the grant of probate or letters of administration, the executor settles all debts, obtains payment of any life insurance policy, and transfers the ownership of any house, shares, or other property the deceased may have had.

Pensions and tax

All pension books and allowance books of the deceased must be returned, either to the DSS or to the issuing office quoted in the payment book; notes of the pension and/or allowance numbers should be carefully kept. If there are any uncashed orders, they must not be cashed after death, even if signed. Any unpaid amounts should be claimed when the book is returned. Any outstanding pension or allowance payments must be specifically claimed by the executors: they will not be paid automatically.

To get any unpaid portions of a war pension, write to the War Pensions Directorate* and claim the amount due, quoting the pension number.

If the deceased had been an officer in one of the armed forces and a pension or allowance was being paid on the basis of war service, the next payment that comes will have to be returned, uncashed, to the issuing office. Send with it a note of the place and date of death, and claim any amount that has become due in the period from the last payment to the death.

If income tax was being deducted from the dead person's salary under the pay-as-you-earn scheme, a refund of tax may be due, depending on the date of death and the tax paid up to then. You will have to apply to the inspector of taxes for the area where the deceased's tax affairs were dealt with; if no one contacts him or her about a refund, the inspector of taxes will not do anything about it. (The executors will hear from the collector of taxes if there is any tax to be paid.)

A widow gets a bereavement allowance (as well as a single person's allowance) to set against her income from the date of her husband's death to the end of the tax year in which he died and for the following tax year (unless she remarries before the new tax year begins). The amount of the widow's bereavement allowance is equal to the difference between the single person's allowance and the married man's allowance.

When independent taxation for husbands and wives was introduced at the beginning of the tax year 1990-91, the system of allowances changed. If a wife dies the husband carries on getting the married couple's tax allowance for the year on top of his own personal allowance. If a husband dies, his widow can get any of the married couple's allowance not used against his income up to the date of his death; and after his death she will get the widow's bereavement allowance plus the additional personal allowance if she has a child living with her, all in addition to her own personal allowance.

The Inland Revenue leaflet IR45 *What happens when someone dies* gives a brief outline of tax matters after a death.

Home and possessions

Responsibility for a house or flat may need to be transferred to the name of another person. Relatives who were living with the deceased in rented accommodation should seek advice about their rights from the local Citizens Advice Bureau or solicitor.

Depending on income and circumstances, a widow or widower may be eligible for Housing Benefit paid through the local authority to assist with rent or council tax. A DSS leaflet RR1 *Help with housing costs* is available at some post offices, and a more detailed explanation is given in leaflet RR4 *Housing benefit new rules*, available at local council offices.

If the telephone was in the name of the deceased, the area telephone manager should be notified, and the service transferred to another name or terminated. A request should be made for the account up to the time of death to be rendered, so that the debt can be paid from the estate. Similarly, requests should be made to gas and electricity authorities for meters to be read and accounts to be submitted; these accounts must also be transferred to another name.

Should a home help or meals-on-wheels have been supplied, the local authority social services department must be notified, and any loaned aid or appliance returned. Library books, records and video tapes should be returned to the respective libraries. If a house or flat has to be cleared quickly, any furniture not required can be offered to a local dealer or put in an auction sale; a number of second-hand or antique dealers offer house clearance services – see local advertisments or *Yellow Pages*. The agreement should ensure that the house is left completely empty, and clean. Sometimes, especially after the sudden death of someone who lived alone, there is an urgent need for drastic cleaning of floors, carpets, bedding, furniture or curtains. Specialist contract cleaners will offer a service to do this: again, see the local telephone book or *Yellow Pages*; funeral directors can often advise.

Local charity shops are glad to receive saleable items, although they must be delivered to the charity concerned at the donor's expense. If the local authority refuse department has to make a special collection, a charge may be made for this service. When a death is announced in local papers, second-hand clothing dealers sometimes call and offer to buy the deceased's clothes: this is an easy way to get rid of unwanted items, but very little will be offered for them. Check all pockets, bags, cases etc. before disposing of them. Other unwanted possessions can also be advertised for sale locally, offered to a dealer or second-hand shop, or given to a charity.

Papers

Various documents will need to be sorted out and examined, and action taken about them. The deceased's medical card should be taken to the registrar when registering the death; if this was not done, it should be sent to the registrar as soon as possible. A rail season ticket should be taken to the station where it was issued, together with proof of death or probate, and a refund claimed. There is no refund for unused railcards. London underground or bus season tickets may be surrendered at any underground station, or posted to the commercial office of London Regional Transport★. A refund may be made from the last day of use if a death certificate is produced, otherwise from the date of surrender. Refunds are made to the widow or widower with no formality; an executor may claim the refund on production of proof of probate or letters of administration, or on producing a solicitor's letter authorising payment.

Passports should be returned to the Passport Office★, or to any of the regional passport offices, together with a letter of explanation. If requested, passports will be returned after cancellation; joint passports must be suitably amended.

If the deceased owned a car, once the new ownership of the car has been settled, the top part of the registration document should be given to the new owner/keeper, and the bottom part sent to the Driver and Vehicle Licensing Centre★, so that the change of ownership can be recorded and a new registration document issued. The deceased's car insurance company should be notified immediately.

For all other insurance policies in the name of the deceased, the relevant companies should be notified, the policies cancelled or amended, and any appropriate refunds claimed.

Claiming money due

Clubs and associations to which the dead person belonged should be told of the death and any unwanted subscriptions cancelled. There may be a refund to claim on unexpired memberships.

To claim on a life insurance policy, send the policy to the company together with the standard death certificate. A policy made 'in trust' for the widow/widower or other named beneficiary bypasses probate, and payment can be made to the beneficiary straightaway. In all other cases, payment may be delayed until probate is grated. If this is longer than two months after the date of death, the insurance company must add interest, at the current market rate, from then until the payment is made.

A number of employers have a life insurance scheme that pays out a lump sum on the death of an employee. And most company pension schemes provide either a cash sum or a pension (sometimes both) for dependants. Find out from the dead person's last employers whether any such payments are now due.

Various societies, professional bodies, trade unions and ex-service organisations run benevolent schemes for the dependants of their members or of people who qualify within the scope of the organisation. The bereaved person should get in touch with the secretary of any organisation related to his or her late spouse's activities to find out which benevolent schemes might be available.

CHAPTER 21

Pensions and other state benefits

Following the death of a spouse or close relative, you may become eligible for certain payments from the state.

The Department of Social Security administers all Social Security benefits. It issues explanatory leaflets for different categories of people and situations – for example, on widow's benefits – and these are available free at any Social Security office. (A list of relevant DSS leaflets is given on page 148.) Or dial 0800 666555 to get the free Social Security telephone information service.

Some benefits are paid only to the dependants of those who had paid, or had credited to them, National Insurance contributions during their lifetime.

You are not expected to know what contributions have been paid or credited when you apply for any benefits. The DSS keeps records of everyone's contributions.

The number of contributions required varies according to the type of benefit claimed. When the number of contributions does not fully qualify for certain benefits, a reduced rate may be paid.

If you need to find out about claiming any benefits after someone has died abroad, write to the overseas branch of the Department of Social Security★.

Help with funeral expenses

The state death grant was abolished in April 1987. In its place, a person responsible for meeting funeral expenses who does not have enough money to do so can apply to the Social Fund which is part of the Social Security system.

Payment can be claimed for the reasonable expense of a funeral in the UK: a hearse and one car, a standard coffin, the services of funeral director and bearers, cemetery or crematorium fees, church, minister's and organist's fees, and all arrangement costs incurred by the funeral director. The payment can also cover the cost of bringing the body home from any place within the UK where death occurred, the return fare for one person's journey either to register the death or to attend the funeral (but not both), the cost of one floral tribute, and up to £75 for special religious costs (such as carrying the coffin into church the night before a funeral). Claims should be made before or within three months of the funeral by completing Form **SF200**, available at DSS offices or from funeral directors.

The Social Fund payment is made only to someone who is (or whose partner is) getting Income Support, Family Credit, Housing Benefit or Disability Working Allowance, and who is responsible for arranging and paying for the funeral: it is irrelevant whether or not the deceased was eligible for these benefits. There must be no cash or other assets of the deceased available without grant of probate or letters of administration, and savings of the applicant will be taken into account – for current amounts, see SF200. Any money payable from insurance policies, charities or personal gifts will be deducted from the payment made.

Any payment made by the state for funeral expenses has to be paid back, in whole or in part, from the estate of the deceased (other than the house and personal belongings left to a widow or widower or relatives) if sufficient funds are eventually available.

Widow's benefit

Widow's benefit is an omnibus term used by the Department of Social Security for a number of payments to which a woman may become entitled following her husband's death. A widow qualifies only if her husband's National Insurance contribution record satisfies the appropriate conditions; her own contributions do not count.

A woman can claim widow's benefit only if she was married to a man at the date of his death. If the marriage had been annulled or dissolved by divorce, the woman is not regarded as his lawful widow. But if the couple were in the process of getting divorced, a woman counts as having been married up to the point where the decree absolute is pronounced. If she marries again while under the age of 60, she loses her widow's benefit from her previous marriage.

A widow does not apply specifically for any one benefit but makes her claim on a detailed form (Form **BW1**), available at any Social Security office or by applying for it on Form **BD8**, on the back of the special copy of the death certificate, supplied free by the registrar when the death is registered. On form BW1 she is asked to give particulars of herself and her late husband and of any children under the age of 19.

She should send off the form as soon as possible, and not later than 12 months after her husband's death in order not to lose any of the benefits. If she can send her marriage and birth certificates too, this will help to speed up the process. It is not necessary to obtain replacement certificates if the originals cannot be found.

A widow who qualifies for benefit can be paid by a book of weekly orders, cashable at a post office, or choose to be paid four-weekly or quarterly in arrears directly into a bank or Girobank account or a national savings bank or building society investment account.

She will be asked to make this choice when filling out application form BW1. Weekly orders are valid for three months; if not cashed within that time, a replacement order must be requested and, if not cashed within 12 months, the benefit of the appropriate order is lost.

Widow's benefit is not affected by any earnings a widow may have or income from investments. It is, however, subject to income tax and may be affected by other Social Security benefits payable to her or similar payments out of public funds, such as a War Widow's Pension or a training allowance.

If her late husband's contributions were insufficient for her to receive the full, or any, widow's benefit, she will be informed in writing. She has a right of appeal to the Social Security appeal tribunal if she disagrees with the decision. This is explained in the notification, and a Citizens Advice Bureau can be asked about the procedure.

If a widow under 60 remarries she loses all entitlement to widow's benefits based on her previous husband's contribution record. A widow under 60 also loses her widow's benefits if she lives with a man as his wife, but can claim again once the cohabitation ends.

Social Security benefits are reviewed by the government at least once a year. The current amounts for the benefits described in the following pages are on pages 146–7.

Widow's Payment

A widow under the age of 60 or whose husband was not getting a retirement pension when he died may get a tax-free lump sum of £1,000, provided his contribution record entitles her to it.

Widow's Pension

A widow without children may receive a weekly pension, depending on her age and on her husband's contribution record.

Contribution requirements

The requirements for a Widow's Pension are that the husband had paid 50 class 1, 2 or 3 contributions at any time before 6 April 1975 or had paid contributions on earnings of at least 50 times the lower earnings limit for the payment of contributions in any one tax year from 6 April 1975 to 5 April 1978 or had paid contributions on earnings of at least 52 times the weekly lower earnings limit for the payment of contributions in any one tax year from 6 April 1978.

For benefit to be paid at the standard rate, the husband must have paid or been credited with contributions equivalent to the level of contributions paid on earnings of at least the minimum specified level (currently, 52 times the weekly lower earnings limit) in a specified number of tax years during his working life.

The husband's working life is normally taken to be the number of complete tax years in the period from 6 April before his 16th birthday to 5 April before his death, or before he reached the age of 65 if earlier. If he was already contributing to the insurance scheme before 5 July 1948, however, the period will count from the tax year in which he entered insurance or 6 April 1936, whichever is later. If he was over 16 on 5 July 1948 and entered insurance on or after that date, the period for the calculation of his working life will begin on 6 April 1948.

The number of years required for a standard rate of basic pension is calculated as follows:

	number of years required
2 to 10 years in working life	the number of years of the working life, minus 1
11 to 20 years in working life	the number of years of the working life, minus 2
21 to 30 years in working life	the number of years of the working life, minus 3
31 to 40 years in working life	the number of years of the working life, minus 4
over 40 years in working life	the number of years of the working life, minus 5

If the husband hadn't paid enough years of contributions, his widow will get a pension reduced in proportion to the number of years of contributions paid, as long as at least a quarter of the number of qualifying years has been achieved.

SERPS or State Earnings Related Pensions
As well as the standard Widow's Pension, a widow may also get an additional (earnings-related) pension based on her husband's earnings as an employed person from April 1978. This pension will be worked out according to a sliding scale revised annually, and published in DSS leaflets **NP45** and **NP46**. If he was a member of a contracted-out occupational pension scheme, part of his widow's additional pension will be payable by that scheme.

Widow under 60 without dependent children
The pension a widow gets depends on her age at the time of her husband's death. (Different rules apply for deaths before April 1988.)

A widow under the age of 45 at that time does not get a Widow's Pension.

A woman who was 45 or over but under 55 when her husband died gets a Widow's Pension calculated on a sliding scale according to her age. This scale starts at 30 per cent of the standard rate for a woman aged 45 at that time and goes in seven per cent steps, so that a widow aged 54 when her husband died gets 93 per cent of the standard rate.

A widow who is 55 or over but under 60 at the time of her husband's death gets the full standard rate of basic pension.

Widow over 60

If a woman is 60 or over at the time of her husband's death and they had both been drawing the retirement pension, she can apply for her retirement pension to be changed to the rate for a widow. She may also be entitled to extra basic pension if her husband had deferred his retirement after he was 65. In addition, she will receive half any graduated pension he was getting.

If a widow is already drawing a retirement pension based on her own contributions but a pension based on her late husband's contributions would be at a higher rate than her own, her pension can be replaced by one based on his.

A widow can inherit the whole of her late husband's basic and SERPS pension. If she is entitled to a retirement pension based on her own contributions, she can add the two retirement pensions together. The sum of the basic pensions is, however, limited to the full rate of basic pension for a single person, and the SERPS pensions to the maximum that a single contributor could have earned from April 1978.

A man whose wife dies when they are both over retirement age can draw a pension derived partly from her contribution record and partly from his own, in exactly the same way as a widow can do, up to the same maximum.

A woman who is not yet drawing retirement pension when her husband dies may qualify for a Widow's Pension, even if she goes on working. Once she has retired, or reaches the age of 65, she inherits half her husband's graduated pension to add to her retirement pension as well as any of her own.

Widow with dependent children

From the date of her husband's death, a widow with dependent children can claim Widowed Mother's Allowance. As well as getting a weekly sum for herself, she will also get an additional allowance for each child under school-leaving age, or who is under 19 and a full-time student or apprentice, or whose school-ing or apprenticeship has been interrupted because of illness. A widow can only claim the extra allowance for a child who was or would have been treated as part of her late husband's family, and normally only for a child living with her.

Widowed Mother's Allowance is also paid to a widow who is expecting a child by her late husband. Once the child is born she will also get an additional amount for the child.

A widow continues to get the widowed mother's personal allowance if any child over 16 but under 19 who has left school is still living with her; she does not get an additional allowance for the child. A widow who is under 45 at the time when her children cease to qualify her for Widowed Mother's Allowance then gets nothing. A widow who by that time is over 45 and under 60 gets the appropriate Widow's Pension for her age then.

War Widow's Pension

If her husband had been in the armed forces and his death could be attributed to his military service, or he had been drawing war pension constant attendance allowance, the widow should write to the War Pensions Directorate* explaining the circumstances fully, and asking if she is entitled to a War Widow's Pension.

Other state benefits

A widow (or anyone else) whose income and savings are below certain levels may be able to claim benefits to top up her income. Advice can be obtained from agencies such as the Citizens Advice Bureau, as well as the DSS.

Income Support

A widow who doesn't work or works for fewer than 16 hours a week and whose savings total less than £8,000 can claim Income Support if her weekly income is below a specified amount. This varies depending on her circumstances, i.e. her age, whether she has dependent children and, if so, how old they are, whether she is disabled or suffers from a chronic illness, whether she has a mortgage to pay and so on. An explanatory leaflet (**1SI**) contain-ing a basic claim form is available at post offices or from the DSS.

Family Credit

A widow who works for 16 hours a week or more, has dependent children and whose savings total less than £8,000 can claim Family Credit if her weekly income is below a certain amount. How much she gets will depend on the number and ages of her children and her income. An explanatory leaflet (**FC1**) which includes a claim form is available at post offices or from the local DSS office.

Housing Benefit

A widow whose savings are less than £16,000 will be able to claim Housing Benefit to help her pay her rent and Council Tax if her income is below a certain amount which varies according to circumstances. Claim forms and information are available from local authority offices.

Industrial Death Benefit

If someone dies as the result of an accident at work or one of the prescribed industrial diseases, it makes no difference to the benefits that can be claimed, except for widows, who may get the full amount of widow's benefits no matter how few National Insurance contributions her husband had paid.

Dependants of people who died before 11 April 1988 could claim Industrial Death Benefit but this cannot be claimed in respect of deaths after this date.

Orphans

A person who takes into the family an orphaned child may be entitled to a Guardian's Allowance. Although the payment is called a Guardian's Allowance, it is not necessary to assume legal guardianship to qualify. Usually the allowance is paid only when both parents are dead, but it can sometimes be paid after the death of one parent – for instance, where the other is missing or cannot be traced, or where the parents were divorced and the other is neither maintaining the child nor subject to any liability for maintenance. The allowance is not awarded unless one of the child's parents was a British subject or had been resident in this country for a specified length of time. It is paid only if the guardian qualifies for child benefit for the child.

Application for a Guardian's Allowance should be made on Form **BG1**, which can be obtained from any Social Security office. A claim should be submitted as soon as possible after the child joins the family, otherwise the guardian may lose some benefit.

When there is no one to take charge of a child, the local authority Social Services department should be told; it will then assume responsibility for the child. If at all possible, children of the same family are kept together.

Widows and National Insurance contributions

A woman who, immediately before her husband died, had full liability for National Insurance contributions (that is, she was required to pay standard rate class 1 contributions when employed and class 2 contributions when self-employed) continues to do so as a widow.

However, if she was paying reduced-rate class 1 contributions when employed immediately prior to the date her husband died, she continues to have reduced liability while she gets widow's benefit. If she doesn't, she will have reduced liability until the end of the tax year (5 April) in which her husband died if he died before 1 October or until the end of the following tax year if he died on or after 1 October. If she changes from reduced-rate to full-rate liability (at any time) she cannot then change back.

There is no liability for a woman to pay any National Insurance contributions after she reaches the age of 60.

Leaflet **NI 51** gives full details of the contribution position of widows and how payment of full or reduced contributions may affect entitlement to National Insurance benefits. A copy of the leaflet is issued to newly widowed women; any woman in doubt about her pension can ask the staff at her local Social Security office for further information and advice. If there is a significant gap in her recent contributions record, she may be able to fill this by making voluntary (class 3) contributions now.

A widow who has responsibilities at home, such as bringing up a child under 16, can have her future right to a basic pension on her own contributions record protected without the need to pay voluntary contributions. She cannot qualify for this protection, however, for any tax year during which she has retained the right to pay reduced-rate contributions. Leaflet **NP 27**, *Looking after someone at home*, gives further details.

NATIONAL INSURANCE BENEFITS: AMOUNTS

The 1993/4 weekly amounts payable for the benefits described in the preceding pages are as follows (DSS leaflet **NI 196** should be consulted for relevant updates):

Widow's benefit

widow's payment	£1,000
widow's full-rate pension	£56.10
widowed mother's allowance	£56.10
plus for each child	£10.95
plus for each child eligible for the higher rate of Child Benefit	£9.80

Family Credit

The maximum amount of Family Credit is payable if your net income is less than £69 per week, but it is worth claiming if your weekly income (not counting child benefit) is less or not much more than:

for one child   £144 if under age 11
£154 if aged 11 to 15
£160 if aged 16 or 17
£173 if aged 18

(For amounts payable for additional children, see the scale in DSS leaflet **FC1**)

The **maximum payment per week** is:

adult credit   £42.50
child credit   £10.75 if under age 11
£17.85 if aged 11 to 15
£22.20 if aged 16 or 17
£31.00 if aged 18

Income Support
The weekly personal *allowances* are:

under 18 (usual rate if eligible)	£26.45
under 18 (in special circumstances if eligible)	£34.80
18 to 24	£34.80
25 or over	£44.00
couple (both under 18)	£52.40
couple (both over 18)	£69.00

plus for each dependent child:	
aged under 11	£15.05
aged 11 to 15	£22.15
aged 16 or 17	£26.45
aged 18	£34.80

The weekly *premiums* for people in certain circumstances are:

family   £9.65

one parent   £4.90

	Single	Couple
pensioner	£17.30	£26.25
enhanced pensioner	£19.30	£29.00
higher pensioner	£23.55	£33.70
disability (under 60 and getting DLA or DWA, IVB, SDA or mobility supplement)	£18.45	£26.45
severe disability (single)	£33.70	
severe disability (couple where one qualifies)		£33.70
severe disability (couple where both qualify)		£67.40
disabled child		£18.45
carer		£11.95

APPLICATION FORMS FOR GRANTS, ALLOWANCES AND PENSIONS

BD8	from registrar, on back of certificate of registration/notification of death	to apply for form BD1 and for form BW1, for Social Security benefits
SF200	from a DSS office and from funeral directors	to claim payment for funeral expenses
BW1	from a DSS office, or by sending form BD8	to claim widow's benefits
NI105	from a DSS office	to apply for payment of benefit direct into banks or building societies
BG1	from a DSS office	to apply for Guardian's Allowance for the support of an orphan
FC1	from a DSS office and post offices	to apply for Family Credit
1SI	from a DSS office and post offices	to apply for Income Support

LEAFLETS ISSUED BY THE DSS

D 49	What to do after a death

about payments and qualifications:

NP 45	A guide to widow's benefits
NI 14	Guardian's Allowance
NI 196	Social Security benefit rates, earnings rules and National Insurance contribution rates
NI 105	Payment direct into banks or building societies: retirement pensions and widow's benefits
NP 46	Retirement pensions – a guide
FB 2	Which benefit?
FB 6	Retiring?
FB 27	Bringing up children?
CH 11	One-parent benefit
1S I	Income Support – cash help
FC 1	Family Credit
MPL 152	War widows: war pensions, allowances and welfare services
MPL 154	Rates of war pensions and allowances

about paying National Insurance contributions:

NI 51	National Insurance for widows
NI 42	National Insurance voluntary contributions
NI 27A	National Insurance contributions for people with small earnings from self-employment
NI 255	National Insurance contributions: direct debit
NP 28	More than one job? your class 1 NI contributions

These leaflets are available free from any DSS office.

INLAND REVENUE LEAFLETS
Leaflet IR 45 about what happens when someone dies and leaflet IR 23 about income tax and widows are available free from tax offices.

CHAPTER 22

BEFORE YOUR OWN DEATH

A PRINTED form *Instructions for my next of kin and executors upon my death* is available for 25p (in stamps) from Age Concern England*. On this, you can put down details of yourself that may be useful when your death is being registered (such as your place of birth, NHS number, details of parents and spouse/s), and information about your possessions, insurance policies, employer, with spaces for the names and addresses of relevant people such as solicitor, bank manager, accountant and tax inspector. You can say on it where you keep important documents, not only your will, but birth certificate, marriage certificate, deeds of house, certificates, savings account books. Your wishes regarding your funeral can also be recorded on the form.

Make sure that your family or whoever you live with, or your executors, know about the form and where it is kept.

The Age Concern form is not intended to take the place of a will and says 'you are strongly advised to make a will even if you do not own very much'.

The property of a person who dies intestate (that is, without leaving a valid will) is divided among the family according to the intestacy rules; if he or she has no close relatives, it may all go to the Crown.

Consumers' Association's *Wills and Probate* explains how to make a will, what to say in it, how to have it witnessed, and what happens if there is no will.

It is quite customary to put into a will whether you wish your body to be cremated or buried, but it is important to let your family know because there may be a delay before the will is read.

Making your wishes about organ donation known

The donor card

Anyone who would like any part of his or her body to be used to save or prolong someone's live should complete one of the small red and blue donor cards available at GPs' surgeries, hospitals, clinics, dispensing chemists and social security offices. This card should be carried with you at all times. It is important, however, to discuss your wishes with your nearest kin and your GP and let them know that you have signed a donor card as evidence of your willingness to let parts of your body be used for the treatment of others. If you go into hospital as an in-patient, be sure to tell the ward sister or other senior members of staff that you are a potential donor. (See also **Chapter 4**.)

Eyes

Corneal donation alone can be considered when someone dies at home or in hospital after any illness. In this case it is important to let the GP or hospital know that the person who dies wanted corneal donation to take place.

If you specifically want the cornea of your eyes to be used, you can get in touch with the Royal National Institute for the Blind's★ prevention of blindness services co-ordinator. You will be sent a multi-organ donor card to sign and keep, a leaflet giving information on what is involved, and a letter with details of the appropriate hospital to be contacted in your area.

The body

Before expressing a formal wish that your whole body be used for anatomical examination and medical education, you should discuss the matter with your family and next of kin, and also tell your executors, because they will have to act quickly after you have died.

To make the arrangements, you should contact the professor of anatomy at your nearest medical school or HM Inspector of Anatomy at the Department of Health★. In Scotland the Scottish Home and Health Department★ can provide information.

Requesting cremation

People who wish to be cremated can register with the Cremation Society* under a scheme which the Society calls FATE ('Funeral Arrangements for use by Trustees and Executors'). The registration fee is £10. The particulars you give about yourself (doctor, next of kin, executor, solicitor, life insurance policies, whereabouts of your will, type of funeral service you would like, any medical donor bequests) are recorded and a copy sent to you, with an identity card for you to carry which asks that the Cremation Society be informed before any funeral arrangements are made on your death.

A note to executors or family on a piece of plain paper is just as valid, albeit less formal. But even if you leave specific instructions that you want – or do not want – your body to be cremated, there is no legal obligation on executors or next of kin to carry out your wishes.

Pre-payment for the funeral

An increasing number of people choose to make arrangements personally for their own funerals, paying for the expenses to be incurred in advance. A number of pre-payment schemes are currently available, all offering a selection of funeral types and prices. Almost all the schemes offer at least three choices:

- *basic*: a simple, basic funeral service which covers all the funeral director's charges and disbursements paid to crematoria, minister, doctors etc. Such plans usually specify cremation, but can be changed to burial, which may involve an extra charge (burial is normally more expensive than cremation)
- *standard*: the funeral director's 'normal' service, as above, but including a better-quality coffin, a limousine for mourners, disbursements covering either burial or cremation, and often other services
- *superior*: a service as above but including a solid wood coffin, two or more limousines for mourners, all disbursements and other services.

These plans are marketed under various names, according to the organisation which provides them. Normally, funeral directors are agents for only one scheme (which will include at least the three categories above), and several sources should be investigated before a choice is made. There are currently at least five different schemes available in the UK, one of which is organised by the National Association of Funeral Directors*. Leaflets and brochures explaining all the schemes are available from funeral directors, or by response to advertisements in the media.

Payment is made either by a lump sum or by instalments. The lump sum payment for the cheapest version of all the schemes currently on offer is in the region of £800 (1994), and covers the total cost of the funeral, no matter how much prices may rise. Instalments are payable over a number of years, which vary according to the scheme chosen. Should death occur before instalments are fully paid, a sum equal to the number of instalments due will need to be paid by the executors. Proceeds are paid into a trust fund which is administered by independent, reputable authorities.

It is normal for a funeral director (not necessarily the one consulted) to be chosen at the time of taking out the plan; when death occurs, the central office of the company promoting the plan is informed, which then instructs the funeral director to carry out the funeral arrangements.

ADDRESSES

There are many organisations which exist to offer help and support to bereaved individuals and families. We include details for some of those below, along with the addresses and telephone numbers for other organisations mentioned in the text.

Age Concern England
Astral House
1268 London Road
Norbury
London SW16 4ER
Tel 081–679 8000

Association of Charity Officers
c/o RICS Benevolent Fund
1st Floor
Tavistock House North
Tavistock Square
London WC1H 9RJ
Tel 071–383 5557

British Humanist Association
14 Lamb's Conduit Passage
London WC1R 4RH
24-hour helpline (0608) 652063

British Organ Donors Society
(BODY)
Balsham
Cambridge CB1 6DL
Tel (0223) 893636

Cancer Relief Macmillan Fund
15–19 Britten Street
London SW3 3TZ
Tel 071–351 7811

Compassionate Friends
53 North Street
Bristol BS3 1EN
Tel (0272) 539639

Cremation Society
Brecon House
16–16a Albion Place
Maidstone
Kent ME14 5DZ
Tel (0622) 688292/3

Cruse – Bereavement Care
Cruse House
126 Sheen Road
Richmond
Surrey TW9 1UR
Tel 081–940 4818
Helpline 081–332 7227 (Mon to Fri,
9.30–5pm)

Driver and Vehicle Licensing Centre
(DVLC)
Swansea SA99 1AR

Fisheries Inspectorate
Ministry of Agriculture
Nobel House
17 Smith Square
London SW1P 3HK
Tel 071–238 5815

Foundation for the Study of Infant
Death (SID)
35 Belgrave Square
London SW1X 8QB
Tel 071–235 0965
24-hour helpline 071–235 1721

General Register Office
Postal Application Section
Office of Population Censuses and
Surveys
Smedley Hydro
Trafalgar Road
Birkdale
Southport PR8 2HH
Tel 051–471 4200

General Register Office (Scotland)
New Register House
Edinburgh EH1 3YT
Tel 031–334 0380

Home Office
D Division
Room 1183
Queen Anne's Gate
London SW1H 9AT
Tel 071–273 3776

HM Inspector of Anatomy
Department of Health
Wellington House
133–155 Waterloo Road
London SE1 8UG
Tel 071–972 2000

Institute of Family Therapy
43 New Cavendish Street
London W1M 7RG
Tel 071–935 1651

Iris Fund for the Prevention of
Blindness
Ground Floor
York House
199 Westminster Bridge Road
London SE1 7UT
Tel 071–928 7743/7919

Jewish Bereavement Counselling
Service
I Cyprus Gardens
London N3 1SP
Tel 071–387 4300 ext. 227
*(North, south-east London and Redbridge
only; advice on support in other areas)*

Lesbian and Gay Bereavement
Project
Vaughan Williams Centre
Colindale Hospital
London NW9 5HG
Tel 081–200 0511
Helpline 081–455 8894

London Regional Transport
55 Broadway
London SW1H OBD
Tel 071–222 5600

Memorial Advisory Bureau
139 Kensington High Street
London W8 6SX
Tel 071–937 0052

Miscarriage Association
c/o Clayton Hospital
Northgate
Wakefield
West Yorkshire WF1 3JS
Tel (0924) 200799

National Association of Funeral
Directors
618 Warwick Road
Solihull
West Midlands B91 1AA
Tel 021–711 1343

National Association of Memorial
Masons
Crown Buildings
High Street
Aylesbury
Bucks HP20 1SL
Tel (0296) 434750

National Association of Widows
54–57 Allison Street
Digbeth
Birmingham B5 5TH
Tel 021–643 8348

National Council for Voluntary
Organisations
Regents Wharf
8 All Saints Street
London N1 9RL
Tel 071–713 6161

National Secular Society
702 Holloway Road
London N19 3NL
Tel 071–272 1266

Natural Death Centre
20 Heber Road
London NW2 6AA
Tel 081–208 2853

Overseas Branch of the Department
of Social Security
Longbenton
Newcastle upon Tyne NE98 1YX

Passport Office
Clive House
70 Petty France
London SW1H 9HD
Tel 071–279 3434

Rationalist Press Association
88 Islington High Street
London N1 8EW
Tel 071–430 1371

The Registrar General (Northern
Ireland)
Oxford House
49–55 Chichester Street
Belfast BT1 4HL
Tel (0232) 526947

Registrar General of Shipping and
Seamen
Block 2
Government Buildings
St Agnes Road
Gabalfa
Cardiff CF4 4YA
Tel (0222) 586000

Royal National Institute for the Blind
224 Great Portland Street
London W1N 6AA
Tel 071–388 1266

Samaritans
10 The Grove
Slough
Berkshire SL1 1QP
Tel (0753) 532713

Scottish Home and Health
Department
St Andrew's House
Edinburgh EH1 3DE
Enquiries 031–556 8400

South Place Ethical Society
Conway Hall
25 Red Lion Square
London WC1R 4RL
Tel 071–831 7723

Stillbirth and Neonatal Death Society
(SANDS)
28 Portland Place
London W1N 4DE
Tel 071–436 7940
Helpline 071–436 5881

War Pensions Directorate
Norcross
Blackpool FY5 3WP
Helpline (0253) 858858

INDEX